WATCH EVERYTHING

WATCH EVERYTHING

A JUDICIAL MEMOIR WITH A POINT OF VIEW

Charles A. Shaw

iUniverse LLC
Bloomington

Watch Everything
A Judicial Memoir with a Point of View

iUniverse books may be ordered through booksellers or by contacting:

iUniverse LLC
1663 Liberty Drive
Bloomington, IN 47403
www.iuniverse.com
1-800-Authors (1-800-288-4677)

Because of the dynamic nature of the Internet, any web addresses or links contained in this book may have changed since publication and may no longer be valid. The views expressed in this work are solely those of the author and do not necessarily reflect the views of the publisher, and the publisher hereby disclaims any responsibility for them.

Any people depicted in stock imagery provided by Thinkstock are models, and such images are being used for illustrative purposes only.
Certain stock imagery © Thinkstock.

ISBN: 978-1-4917-1148-4 (sc)
ISBN: 978-1-4917-1149-1 (hc)
ISBN: 978-1-4917-1150-7 (e)

Library of Congress Control Number: 2013918808

Printed in the United States of America.

iUniverse rev. date: 10/23/2013

CONTENTS

Watch Everything: A Judicial Memoir with a Point of View by Federal Judge Charles Shaw reflects a respected jurist's great enthusiasm for protecting the rights, privileges and obligations of citizens accused of criminal violations while at the same time preserving the fundamental precept of the American system of justice: those guilty must be adequately punished.

Shaw, a gifted wordsmith, has woven love of family and devotion to the legal profession into an informative, sometimes humorous narrative that recognizes and credits his parents for instilling in him the moral and religious values making him what he has become.

Reading the story of Shaw's successful supersonic rise from childhood in a segregated St. Louis inner-city neighborhood to his encounters with the intricacies of our judicial system is a sobering experience. The book focuses on his reaching the pinnacle of the legal profession with the help of many individuals who provided invaluable advice and assistance along the way.

Watch Everything is an exceptionally well-written presentation of Shaw's wide experiences with some of the best legal minds in the country. He challenges prevailing concepts that are too often accepted by a naive public, such as that laws and practices prohibiting discrimination against racism, sexism, age and other inequities are no longer necessary.

Watch Everything is an easy read but a seriously provocative, insightful introspective review of the judicial system that makes a compelling case for preserving the basic framework while reforming certain aspects of it.

I recommend the book to those concerned about fairness, justice and equity in our judicial system.

William L. Clay, Sr.
U.S. Congress, Retired

A fascinating, funny inside look at our justice system and an indictment of the process that can deprive people of their right to trial, where non-violent offenders are sentenced too harshly and where prosecutors have more power than presidentially appointed judges.

Edward L. Dowd, Jr.
Dowd Bennett LLP
and Former U.S. Attorney
Eastern District of Missouri

Watch Everything is a powerful and honest memoir about Charles Shaw, an African American; who rose from a teacher to a senior status federal judge. Shaw writes about his boyhood and offers unforgettable portraits of his father, mother and grandmother, and many other people who shaped his early life.

Shaw offers bold and daring criticisms of the inequality in the federal sentencing guidelines and provides a good argument for ending the unfairness. Using many case histories, Judge Shaw sketches his own conflicts with the federal sentencing guidelines and discusses the challenges he faced as a federal judge. Repeatedly, he shows us how the system that considers itself fair, in reality, is itself pernicious.

Watch Everything is thought provoking and compelling. I strongly recommend this book to all who wish to become aware of a roadmap to the making of a federal judge.

Robert L. Williams, Ph.D.
Professor Emeritus
Washington University-St. Louis

To judge, a Judge must first be *judged*. Charles A. Shaw passes all Bars of Humanity and *proves* his case in this memoir—testament to a life well-deployed in *service* to us all.

Bernard Shaw
CNN Anchor Emeritus

Watch Everything offers a clear and understandable vision of the author's remarkable journey to the federal bench. Shaw shows us how family and God provide the strength and fuel to not only dream big, but to persevere and achieve those dreams.

Dwayne Butler, President and CEO
People's Health Centers
St. Louis, Missouri

Watch Everything is a true story about the struggle to succeed. Shaw paved his own way, through determination, perseverance and a relentless desire to survive.

Ronnie L. White, Retired Judge
Supreme Court of Missouri

Watch Everything by Charles Shaw is humorous yet serious; a "Must Read."

Dr. Henry Givens, Jr.
President Emeritus
Harris-Stowe State University

This book is dedicated to my wife Kay, son Bryan, and daughter-in-law LaMisa. I cherish and appreciate each of you.

Thanks Kay for loving, supporting, inspiring and believing in me. Your smile, tender spirit and positive outlook motivate me in so many ways. I love you to no end.

Thanks Bryan for being the sensitive, friendly and caring man that you have become. When I am measured by you, I am a resounding success. I am proud to be your father. Love, Dad.

Thanks LaMisa for joining our family. Your joy, kindness, enthusiasm and dedication make you a treasure beyond compare. We know that a loving and wonderful lady has joined our clan. Pops loves you, daughter.

With Kay, Bryan and LaMisa

FOREWORD

Watch Everything is an autobiography, highlighting a very distinguished legal career, of an unpretentious, dedicated, undaunted public servant, who describes a journey, told as a human story, from early days in Tennessee, where the laws denied him equal access to public services, to an appearance before the United States Senate Judiciary Committee, as a presidential nominee as United States District Judge for the Eastern District of Missouri, through his term as an active District Judge, until his current status as a Senior United States District Judge. It provides motivation for any reader to imitate the lesson of Machiavelli, in *The Prince*, not to walk in paths beaten by others, and act by imitation, rather, realizing "a person cannot hold strictly to the ways of others or match the ability of those he imitates, a prudent man must always tread the path of great men, and imitate those who have excelled, so that even if his ability does not match theirs, at least he will achieve some semblance of it. He should act like a prudent archer who, knowing the limitation of his bow and judging the target to be too far off, sets his aim still farther off, not to strike so distant a mark, but rather to strike the desired target through the more ambitious aim." The author strikes the mark of an ambitious aim.

The depth of his character is defined by unrelenting love of parents, siblings, collateral family, friends and strong faith, all of which enriched his life from the earliest memories through marriage to precious Kay, law school at Catholic University in Washington, D.C., where he was awarded a full scholarship, private practice of law with a prestigious law firm in St. Louis, Assistant United States Attorney for the Eastern District of Missouri, Circuit Judge for the Twenty-Second Judicial Circuit of Missouri and as a life-tenured United States District Judge for the Eastern District of Missouri. He faced many obstacles in a well-lived life, continuously striving to secure equal justice for all. Charles A. Shaw has lived the American Dream.

This book reveals how a man of humble beginnings worked tirelessly, so others, under the rule of law, would believe the words "all men are created equal" have meaning, and no part of the American Dream should be foreclosed to anyone. It reveals the strength of intentional will, to place before appellate courts, challenges to write the law with reason replacing rigid construction, at risks of personal reprisal. Sometimes, stepping away from "watch everything" must yield to a voice for equal justice.

A life is an accumulation of experiences which influence the character of a person. How many today can write from personal experiences of living at a time in America where a father's warning, "watch everything," and a mother's admonition not to go into a restaurant where only "whites" were to be served? Such experiences can break the will to succeed or be the source of an indomitable force to defy probabilities, and serve at a high level in America's proud judiciary, working from the coming of time when no mother need fear her child will be seen by any man in a lesser state than viewed by the Creator of all.

Humor is the magic that can disarm hostility and restore order in chaotic situations. In the American courtrooms, there is more human drama than the most imaginative writers can fashion. The author is the master in the effective utilization of impromptu comments that remove the venom from unprofessional behavior, which appropriately re-directs interrogations designed to take fact-finders away from the truth, rather than to it, and which draws personnel from other chambers for instruction, and occasional entertainment.

Apparent from a casual read is the careful and generous recitation of quotes of literary scholars, presidents and folk heroes to support particular points. This book takes the reader through visions of a child to the demands placed on a highly motivated jurist, adhering to the high calling of his oath, while searching for the right conclusions, based on the law, the evidence of the case and years of lessons of human and inhuman experiences. There is much to be learned about what is possible in the pursuit of goals that will enhance their lives.

E. Richard Webber
Senior U.S. District Judge
Eastern District of Missouri

PREFACE

My life has been enhanced to an exceptionally positive degree by my family: my wife Kay, son Bryan, my two brothers Alvis and Booker, as well as my parents. They have supported and stood by me in all endeavors. I love them dearly.

There are many books about the law as well as about attorneys and judges. This book, however, tells such a story from my perspective as a St. Louis African-American judge who grew up on the north side of the city, rose through the ranks, attended public schools, and was fortunate beyond my imagination.

Life does not always give us successes but it gives us opportunities to succeed. I had those, and I have also had good fortune. I feel blessed and truly favored, and I know there is a God who looked out for me.

My tenure as a federal district judge in St. Louis has been wonderful and rewarding. There have been highs and lows, but more peaks than valleys. My wonderful Judicial Assistants, Carole Peek and Linda Errante Wehner, have made federal judgeship pleasant. Their support and assistance have been immeasurable. The same can be said for my law clerks, but particularly Susan Heider, who has been with me throughout my judicial tenure. Former Chief U.S. District Judge Carol Jackson pointed this out to me when she said, "Charles, you have been extremely fortunate with an excellent staff." I can't dispute her assertion.

It gives me great pleasure seeing the growth, both personal and professional, of the young lawyers who have come through my office and served as law clerks. I know that they have also helped me grow. Thanks to you all:

Sheila Brennan
Daniel Brown
Lisa Parker Freeman
Keith Grady
Susan Heider
Robin Jefferson Higgins
Anne Maloney
Ebony Woods McCain
Maggie Peters
Lynn Reid
Phyllis Shapiro
Steve Sherman
Craig Simmons
Ken Takahashi
Kirsten Wilkerson

Currently, I am serving the federal courts as a Senior U.S. District Judge. Based on my age and years of service as a federal judge, I became eligible for retirement at full benefits some time ago. Instead of retiring, like many federal judges I chose to continue to work and currently manage a caseload of approximately sixty percent of a full district judge caseload. According to the United States Courts website, "Senior judges, who essentially provide volunteer service to the courts, typically handle 15 percent of the federal courts' workload annually."

When lay people suggested that I was retired and they could not quite comprehend the concept of senior status, they have understood and laughed at my explanation, "I just make cameo appearances." Being on senior status has given me time to reflect on writing this book. I was hesitant, but friends encouraged me to get it on.

Congressman William L. Clay, Sr., retired, was not only key to my appointment to the federal bench but was also instrumental in my writing this book. He told me, "Do not let anyone else write your story.

Write it yourself." Thank you, Congressman Clay, for inspiring me to become the master of my story. Inspiration also came from an African proverb that says, "Until lions have their own historians, tales of the hunt will always glorify the hunter." People should record their own stories, otherwise their histories may be lost or inaccurately written by others who do not share the same point of view. I hope this book will encourage others to write about the events of their lives. As Supreme Court Justice Sonia Sotomayor has noted, "Don't measure yourself by others' expectations or let anyone define your worth." These are my stories from my point of view.

CHAPTER ONE

My Parents

I am deeply grateful that my parents lived long enough to see me ascend to the federal bench. This was particularly true for Dad, because he had worked in the Federal Court and Custom House (the official name of the old federal courthouse building in St. Louis) as a U.S. Customs Inspector for many years and was familiar with the respect that the judges were accorded. My parents had long, love-filled and meaningful lives and had a huge influence on my life and those of my brothers.

My parents: Alvis Shaw, Sr. and Sarah Weddle Shaw

Mother, Sarah Weddle Shaw, who passed away in 2004, was a wonderful mother. Abraham Lincoln said, "All that I am or ever hope to be, I owe to my angel Mother." That statement applies to my feelings about my mother. Sarah Shaw molded, taught and fostered a sense of worth in all of her children. She made her boys into men. An old Jewish proverb says, "God could not be everywhere and therefore he made mothers." Mother raised us with her morals, taught us to love and respect our fellow human beings, and insisted that we take responsibility, have standards and pride, and be understanding and forgiving of others.

God was extremely important in Mother's life. Our family attended church regularly, she sang in the choir for many years, and she made sure that her sons were involved with the church. We sang in the youth choir, attended Sunday school at St. John A.M.E. Church on North Kingshighway Boulevard in the city, and were Boy Scouts. My older brother, Alvis, Jr., and I also took piano lessons from the pastor's wife, Mrs. Hayden, and were frequently in trouble for not practicing. Mother got so many calls from the church about it that she gave Booker, the youngest son, a pass on piano lessons. Ironically, Booker went to college on a music scholarship. Alvis and I did not.

Family was the other important feature of Sarah Shaw's life. Each summer the entire family sojourned to the Weddle homestead in Denmark, Tennessee where Mother's six sisters either lived or likewise brought their families. Like Mother, all of her sisters loved to sing, sang in their church choirs, and many were church pianists.

Out on Grandmother Lela Weddle's 160-acre farm the children laughed, played, worked, prayed and sang together for the entire summer. We were all out of harm's way there in a loving yet disciplined family environment. Although my parents went back and forth to St. Louis, Grandmother who we affectionately called "Mama Lela" was in charge of all activities with the help of three of Mother's sisters who lived nearby.

Mama Lela

Mama Lela was the only grandparent my brothers and I knew, as our other three grandparents were deceased. She ruled the roost and made all the final decisions regarding the farm and its welfare. Also, during the summer she was the disciplinarian of all her grandchildren. If you severely misbehaved, you were directed to go and bring a switch, a small branch from a tree about 1/4 inch in diameter and 36 inches in length. This is what she administered your flogging with, all about your arms, legs and body. My goodness, would it sting and leave welts! God forbid you bring back too small a switch, that meant extra strokes for you.

Mama Lela was a devout Christian, as had been our grandfather, Caul Weddle. The seven sisters were all taught music by their father Caul, who was a church pianist and vocalist. Besides church service on Sunday, there was a service on Wednesday evening. We would ride to church on a dirt road in a wagon pulled by mules. My most vivid recollection of those services involves sitting on the "mourning bench" on Wednesday evenings. Around the age of eleven or twelve, the members' children had to sit on a bench pew facing the congregation while the service was in progress, and the service was significantly directed to those on the bench. The children had to continue to sit there each Wednesday night until they physically showed some manifestation of being embraced by the Holy Spirit. I sat on that mourning bench for three consecutive

Wednesdays until it became apparent that I had to rise, make a few moves, manifest some tears and acknowledge my acceptance of Jesus Christ. After that, no more mourning bench for "the kid."

On the farm we rose early to go bring in the cows from their grazing to the barnyard. We had to help milk the cows and pump water from the well for drinking, cooking and bathing. After eating a hearty breakfast, hot biscuits with molasses, scrambled eggs and bacon, we were off to school with a packed lunch for the first couple of weeks we were there. In that area of Tennessee, the local school year was somewhat disjointed to accommodate planting and harvesting crops. They held school for part of the summer, and we went too. The school was a segregated, one-room wood building that accommodated grades one through eight. It made me feel that we were privileged to have a classroom for each grade in St. Louis.

Alvis, Booker and I were among the youngest of the cousins, so we never did any physically demanding work on the farm as it was beyond our abilities. I do recall feeding the chickens and hogs, picking and shelling peas, shucking corn, and churning milk to make butter and, on Sunday evenings, ice cream. We watched our older and more farm-experienced cousins do the real hard work. They plowed the crop fields using a mule and a steel plow. Years later, my late cousin Van Weddle of Las Vegas, Nevada, would from time to time derisively declare, "Never again will a mule fart in my face!"

The journeys to and from Tennessee were part of the adventure. As many African Americans of my generation know, when you traveled in the 1950s you had with you that ever-present shoe box stuffed with fried chicken, bread, fruit and cake. Blacks were not welcome in restaurants on the highways and food service was an issue on trains and where buses stopped. When we traveled to Tennessee, Mother would prepare shoe boxes full of scrumptious food and lined with wax paper to keep the grease from seeping through the box and maintain some degree of freshness. The food was indeed finger-licking good.

Back in St. Louis, my parents' home was always open to our friends. They all knew they were welcome. Sarah Shaw was a great cook, as was attested to by all our friends as well as Dad's. The kitchen table was long and shaped like a two-sided bar with stools on each side and one at each end. It seated a dozen. When Dad's buddies weren't occupying it, our friends were there awaiting whatever dish Mother prepared. My favorite was her German chocolate cake. Mmm, mmm, good! Our friends' price for admission, however, was a thorough interrogation by Mother as to what they were doing with their lives. She would also inquire in detail about their families. Make no mistake about it, Sarah Shaw was strictly law and order. Brother Booker was fond of joking that when FBI agents finished their training, they could take graduate classes from Mother, especially on interrogation techniques.

It didn't occur to me until years later that Mother made sure our home was open and inviting to all of our friends, and Dad's friends, in part because she wanted to keep tabs on us and have some control over what we were doing. At the time, we just knew that everyone was welcome, and there was always good food and good times to be had at our house.

Making sure that her sons got a good education was extremely important to Mother. She was always reminding us that we needed to do our homework and get good grades, and urging us to plan to go to college. Her mantra was, "You have to get an education. That is something that no one can take away from you." After I was appointed to the state bench in 1987, Shirley Davis, my paralegal in the United States Attorney's Office, told me she asked my mother how she managed to have three successful sons, including two judges. Shirley said my mother responded, "I kept my foot on their heads at all times." She was not joking. Mother was a strict disciplinarian.

Whenever Mother was verbally chastising one of the brothers or our cousin Edison Mosley, who was raised with us as a brother, you added your two cents about the other's bad behavior at your peril. If she thought you were adding fuel to the fire against the miscreant, Mother immediately turned the table on you. We learned to just spectate.

Mother was also wise as to human nature. Sometimes she would say, "You can learn something from a fool." She was telling us to listen to and consider what everyone has to say. If you think the person is inarticulate or awkward, or even stupid, you shouldn't simply write off as useless anything that person says. Everyone has their own viewpoint and ideas. Sometimes nuggets of truth and wisdom can be found where they are least expected. I've particularly tried to keep this saying in mind when dealing with persons who are representing themselves, and even sometimes with lawyers!

Sarah Shaw did have a great sense of humor and was fond of saying to Dad's friends as they left, "Let the door knob hit you where the good Lord split you." The response was always a chuckle. Mother was also fond of telling us, "You can't tell Jesse James how to rob no train." She was telling us that she was in charge and it didn't matter how sound your suggestion was. Although she never told the full joke, we later overheard it, without their knowledge, from Dad's friends. It goes like this: Jesse James was robbing a train and announced that he was going to rob all the women and rape all the men. In an effort to correct Jesse, one of the passengers said, "Don't you have that backwards?" Jesse James responded, "You can't tell Jesse James how to rob no train."

Many of the stories and jokes that I heard Dad tell when I was a child, I heard only because I was listening outside a door when I shouldn't have been. Adult conversations were just that. My family lived by the rule that "children should be seen and not heard," and sometimes we would be pulled aside and reminded of this rule if we had the temerity to try and join in the adults' conversation.

I am very thankful to my dear mother for loving me and for all that she gave me, asking for nothing in return. I hope that I made her proud.

With Mom, wife Kay and Dad

Dad was a different character than Mother, but equally influential in my life. Life for Alvis Shaw, Sr. was very simple: work hard, take care of your responsibilities, know right from wrong, enjoy life and, as he always cautioned when we boys left the house, "Watch everything." Dad was telling us that things outside the home could be dangerous and you could be harmed, so pay attention to your environment and the people around you. In other words, be careful where you go and who you are with.

Dad gave his sons spirit, pride, fortitude, tenacity and belief in ourselves. He believed that there wasn't anything you couldn't do if you worked hard enough at it with your body and mind. Alvis, Sr. also gave his sons a sense of family pride and strength. He was a man of indomitable will. We had no doubt that we came from a long line of spiritually and mentally strong men: his father Lawrence "the Rock," our uncles, and our older cousins. We did not need fictional heroes. Alvis Shaw, Sr. and his brothers were our real life heroes. They were men's men. They were true to family, friends, community, the nation, and their God.

Like Mother who was one of seven sisters, Dad was one of seven brothers, along with three sisters. The only one of his brothers who also lived in St. Louis was Uncle Booker. Uncle Booker always carried a wad of bills in his pocket (credit cards had not yet come into existence), and as soon as he would see you he would ask, "Do you have any money in your pocket?" If your answer was "no," he would pull out and display his wad and bestow a blessing on you, with the admonition to always keep some money in your pocket. He was very generous to his nephews and was much loved in return. Uncle Booker was a sharp dresser and kept a shining new car. When I was twelve years old, he bought me a red wagon in which I hauled groceries from the neighborhood store on Friday evenings and Saturday. He then had me loaning money to his and Dad's friends at twenty-five cents on the dollar for a week. I now realize they didn't need a loan, they just enjoyed seeing me do a business hustle. Uncle Booker was a legend among the Shaw clan for his gregariousness and generosity.

Uncle Booker and Dad

We felt that we grew up with a hero in our home. My brothers and I thought Dad was the best at everything and there was nothing he couldn't do. To us he was witty, charming, handsome, and strong. Very strong. He was John Wayne and David Niven, Sidney Poitier and Dick Gregory, all rolled into one. A force of nature, and a man to be reckoned with.

A fabled story in my family concerns my brother's Oldsmobile 442 convertible, and it reveals something of who Dad was and what we thought of him. I apologize to law enforcement personnel for the content of this story. Boys and girls, ladies and gentlemen, do not try this at home.

The year was 1967, and I was twenty-two. It was a gorgeous, sunny, Saturday fall afternoon. We were all at home, except for Dad, who had gone hunting with Uncle Booker and two of their hunting buddies. Mother, as usual, was in the kitchen cooking, but she needed some essential ingredient. Brother Booker was sent to the store to get the missing staple, and he asked to borrow Alvis, Jr.'s brand new car, the 442. Why Alvis let him drive it, I'll never know. The 1967 Oldsmobile 442 was a muscle car, a high-performance automobile. At that time it was one of the most beautiful and desirable cars, and today it's a collector's item. Alvis loved cars and he had the prettiest one in St. Louis: black on black, with a black convertible top and chrome wheels. Anyone who knew Alvis, Jr. knew that it was clean, too.

So Booker took the car, went to the store, got the groceries, and when he came out the car was gone, stolen! He made frantic calls home and to the police. Coincidentally, Dad and the other hunters were just arriving back at our house as Booker's call came in. They went to pick up Booker and Dad got the story from him. Dad believed that whoever took the car was probably still joyriding around the neighborhood. I believe he looked at his sons and thought, "I've got to do something about this." So he decided to go looking for the car.

The four hunters jumped back into their station wagon and peeled off. Having just returned from hunting, they were packing some heat. They were armed to the teeth. Somewhere around the intersection of Page Boulevard and Taylor Avenue they saw Alvis's car with four young men in it, joyriding just like Dad thought. Dad pulled up next to them and ordered them to pull over. Perhaps the hunters may have displayed a shotgun or three. It was on! The thieves took off like a jet in the 442, with the station wagon chasing, whipping up and down Page, Taylor, Easton, and west to Aubert. The thieves took a wrong turn down a dead-end alley with the hunters right behind. Those young men must've thought they were being chased by some kind of crazy, camouflaged vigilantes because they stopped the car, jumped out of it and fled. They left the car running and in the ignition was a full ring of close to twenty stolen GM car keys.

Imagine our excitement and delight when Dad pulled up to the house in the 442! We all ran off the front porch to get a good look at the car. It was unscathed, with not a scratch, nick, dent, or cut. Then, around the kitchen table, with a little Jack Daniels Black Label, Dad and the hunters laughingly recounted their adventure. Like so many times before, my brothers and I sat and listened. But we weren't really surprised. We already knew we lived with a hero.

Alvis Shaw, Sr. was really the first lawyer in our family. Many of his friends and neighbors, as well as ours, would come to him for advice, help on getting some project done, and assistance in interpreting legal documents. On the block of Greer Avenue where we lived, he was affectionately called the "Mayor of Greer." He inspired his sons to try to help others and to make a difference. Make no mistake about it though, unlike Mother, Dad was no angel. As Abraham Lincoln said, "Folks who have no vices have very few virtues." Alvis Shaw, Sr. enjoyed a drink or two, a smoke or three, and a joke or so.

Almost twenty years ago, shortly after I had taken the federal bench, unbeknownst to me Dad was visiting my chambers while I was in court conducting a hearing. Without any warning, there he came walking into my courtroom through the swinging gate, almost to the podium where the attorneys were addressing me. I halted the proceedings, explaining to the lawyers that this was my father. Dad pointed his finger at me on the bench and blurted out a question: "What are you doing with all that space back there, wasting the government's money?" I sheepishly explained that the government gave me the space, it wasn't my doing. He seemed to think about it for a moment and then, with apparent satisfaction, turned and walked back to the swinging gate. There he hesitated, turned around and said to me, "Tell Judge Tillman to come over Sunday. Your mother is cooking chitterlings," and then he walked on out of the courtroom. Not only did he put short pants on me, a federal judge, but he "ethnicized" the place as well.

Coco Chanel, the great fashion designer and founder of the Chanel brand, once said, "In order to be irreplaceable one must always be different." Dad was such a man, irreplaceable and absolutely different. He was comfortable and forthright no matter where or when, and felt that he was a friend of everyone. We went to the Million Man March on Washington in October 1995. At the time, Dad was a spry eighty-one years old and was difficult to keep up with when the sea of people rolled in. He felt very comfortable and was absolutely positive that he knew many among the million and wanted to say hello to as many of them as he could. If he hadn't had his favorite red cap on we would certainly have lost him in the crowd. We joked that Mother would kill us if we lost him there. Dad was a man who loved people and was loved in return. He made fast friends wherever he ventured.

In 1975, Dad visited Kay and me in Washington, D.C., after we had bought a house in a new development. Early one Saturday morning Dad was not to be found in the house. I looked out the window and there he was on a neighboring family's porch, talking to them. A while later, I looked out and he was at another house doing the same thing, and it continued. After Dad left to return to St. Louis, I joked with friends that he knew more of my neighbors in a weekend than I did after living there for almost a year.

Dad was always forthright and blunt, even within the last year of his life when his mind was clouded with Alzheimer's disease and dementia. One evening when I stopped by to see him, he asked, "What's that other boy's name?" I said, "You mean Booker?" and he said, "Yeah, that's him. He was over here earlier. Where was he going?" I responded, "Home." He paused and then asked, "Where was he coming from?" and I quickly said, "Work." He paused again and asked, "Well, where does he work?" I answered, "He's a judge downtown." Dad rose up off the couch and waved his arm at me saying, "The country's gone to hell." I immediately

11

called Booker and relayed the story, with the conclusion that Dad was very lucid that day.

As Barack Obama said, "We are not sent here to be perfect. We were sent here to make what difference we can." Dad was not perfect, but he certainly made a very great difference in my life.

Growing Up on Greer Avenue

My family lived in the inner city on the north side of St. Louis in a segregated, middle-class neighborhood of tidy, well-kept houses on tree-lined Greer Avenue. Our church was on the next block, the grocery store was about three blocks away, and close to that were the dry cleaners and a Chinese take-out joint. The first school my brothers and I attended, Cote Brilliante Elementary, was about ten blocks away and we walked there. After a couple of years we were transferred to Simmons Elementary, which was slightly closer. I spent most of my time on our block until I was twelve or so, when I was allowed to venture further. Only then did I begin to know people on the next few blocks when I started hauling groceries from the neighborhood store.

Our house was a center of social activity in the neighborhood for adults as well as kids, and was open to all. The first television on the block was at our house, and we would host gatherings for our friends in our home with Mother doing all of the wonderful cooking. I was eight or nine when we got the TV, and us kids watched *Howdy Doody, The Lone Ranger* and *Superman*. Most of the adult social events were either at our house, or at the houses of my parents' friends Ted and Mary Richardson, or Melvin and Minnie Robertson.

The only white people we saw in our neighborhood on a regular basis were the convenience and grocery store owners. Every month or so though, a white gentleman dressed in a white shirt and wearing a tie, sporting a crew cut and glasses while carrying a zipped-up brief case came knocking on our door. He looked like Michael Douglas's character in the movie *Falling Down*. He was an insurance salesman. At that time, black people were only able to buy insurance policies if companies were willing to put someone on the streets in the black neighborhoods going door to door collecting cash premiums and giving out receipts.

We knew all our neighbors and they knew us, and people watched out for each other's children. If you did something wrong away from home, a neighbor would chastise you or even tap you on the behind, and you can be sure the bad news would beat you home. The neighbor would call Mother, and whichever one of us brothers was the offender would get a scolding or an ass-whuppin' when we arrived home, depending on the severity of the transgression. Mother embraced the biblical axiom of "spare the rod and spoil the child," and she would detach the heavy cord from her iron to administer our punishment immediately. Undoubtedly the whippings she gave us would be considered child abuse by today's standards, but it was routine in those days and kept us mostly in line. Even worse was when our conduct was so bad that Mother didn't immediately punish us, but instead would fix us with a disapproving glare and announce the dreaded, "Wait until your father gets home." The mental strain of waiting for Dad to get home, hear of our misconduct, and punish us was almost worse than the eventual whippings we received.

A major rule in our house was to be home by the time the streetlights came on at night, and Alvis, Booker and I would sometimes get in trouble for bending or breaking that rule. We would also be punished for using cuss words, fighting, or for climbing over a neighbor's fence to take a peach off of their peach tree or grapes from their grapevine. Those were hard to resist! There would also be trouble if I was caught playing "the dozens," a game where you called your friend's mama a name, or even just started off a taunt with "yo' mama." We mostly played the dozens for fun or to have a laugh, but if I was upset with someone I might call out a particularly good "yo' mama" crack over my shoulder as I was heading up the front porch steps and into the safety of the house. Unlike me, my older brother Alvis was tough. He was a fighter. When we first moved on the block, some kids brought another kid by who claimed to be the "king of the street" and boasted that he could beat anyone up. Alvis made short work of that kid.

Shooting marbles in a little patch of dirt between the sidewalk and the curb at the street was a favorite pastime when I was a youngster. All of us boys would put our marbles in a circle drawn in the dirt and then take turns using a shooter to knock them out of the circle. The marbles you knocked out of the circle became yours. That was fun until some kids brought heavy steel marbles that knocked almost all of the marbles out at once. Then I went inside unhappy, because I'd lost all my best marbles! Other times, when all the marbles were in the circle, someone would yell, "Squabble!" and then we'd all dive to the ground and try to grab all the marbles we could get. We also played a lot of corkball in the street, using a long thin bat to hit a tennis ball past a player to get points. Every hit counted for a point, and you got to keep hitting until you had three strikes. Sometimes if we didn't have tennis balls, we'd use milk bottle caps. This significantly increased the difficulty because they were harder to hit and didn't go as far.

The family got a second television when I was about thirteen, and Dad fixed up the basement and put the old TV down there. Alvis, Booker and I loved to play cards and would have our friends over to play bid whist into the night. Then we would watch the late night horror movies like *Frankenstein* and *The Mummy*. My brothers and I would stand at the front door watching our friends run home as fast as they could in the dark, scared after watching those movies, and we would laugh because we were already safe at home!

As I got older, I was always interested in trying to earn some spending money. In addition to using the red wagon Uncle Booker gave me to haul groceries, my friends and I would scour the alleys and neighbors' trash cans looking for soda bottles or coat hangers we could turn in at the grocery store or dry cleaners for money. The regular crew for scavenging, as well as hauling groceries, included Mike Thompson, who later became my son's godfather, and the late Danny Crousby. Each of us grew to be successful adults, Mike became a corporate executive and Danny was a commercial property owner and manager. We all had a strong work ethic early on. During the summer we were part-time vendors at Sportsman's Park on North Grand Boulevard (the predecessor to Busch Stadium) selling popcorn, snow cones and soda. I remember the snow cone and soda trays were unbearably heavy. When there were major city events such as the Veiled Prophet parade, the crew sold popcorn, cotton candy or balloons.

But we weren't always all work and no play. Once we sold out of our products, we engaged in the mischief of shooting peas at the people on the floats. This involved a plastic straw and hard, dried peas that we put in our mouths and then blew through the straw with good velocity. Boy was it fun, especially when we shot multiple peas in rapid fire. It was like shooting a machine gun with your mouth. We tried to be practically invisible, stealthily weaving among the parade watchers, discretely taking out our straw guns, taking a shot and promptly reconcealing the weapons. We were like hunters with poison dart guns shooting their prey. Seeing the victims swat their arms or bodies as if they had been stung by a bee gave us great enjoyment, but we knew how they stung, as we would occasionally engage in pea-shooting fights among ourselves. All good things must come to an end, and that's what would happen when a family friend or neighbor was witness to our mischief and made sure the bad news beat us home. Mother would confiscate the easily replaceable weapon and ammunition but, more significantly, she would take another opportunity to employ that vicious ironing cord.

When I was fourteen or fifteen, Alvis and I got real jobs working at the Comet Grill, a restaurant that was popular in the black community. We cooked, cleaned and served customers. Working there was the first time I had ever been in a restaurant, other than getting carry-out from the neighborhood Chinese place. Horseplay was not tolerated at the restaurant, and I learned the meaning of real work. All in all, it was a safe and happy place and time to grow up.

Getting an Education

I enjoyed school as a child, but had developed a terrible stutter by the time I was in the fifth grade. My teacher Anna Wigley was determined to cure me of it. In order to do that, she made me stand and speak to the class on any occasion that she saw fit to call on me, and those occasions were numerous. The resulting laughter from the other students was almost unbearable, but it made me determined to overcome my impediment. It was a "tough love" approach to the problem, but it worked.

Mrs. Wigley cured me of my stutter, and I consider her a hero in my life for having done that. If it had not been for her, I don't know where I would be today. Even now, it is not pleasant to think back on how painful it was to speak when I used to stutter. As a result, I was very reluctant to see the Academy-Award winning movie *The King's Speech* because of its subject matter, although ultimately I was glad I did. It is certain I would not have become a lawyer with my stutter, and after becoming a state court judge in 1987, I let Mrs. Wigley know how much I appreciated her help and what a great influence she was on my life.

Mother was determined that I would get the best education I could. When I was ready to enter high school, she enrolled me at Beaumont High School, even though the neighborhood school was Sumner High, because she thought Beaumont was a better school. I'm sure that if the Voluntary Interdistrict Student Transfer Program had been in effect in the late 1950s, Mother would have had me on a bus to a suburban St. Louis county school. I attended my first two years of high school at Beaumont, but ultimately the school administration figured out I didn't belong there and showed me the door. I was quite unhappy at the time to be leaving friends and my place on the track team where I enjoyed running the 120-yard hurdles, but the move to Sumner High actually turned out to be a very good thing and set in motion a momentous event in my life.

Charles E. Sumner High School was the first high school for African-American students west of the Mississippi River. Sumner had a wonderful teaching staff of highly qualified African-American educators, in part because in St. Louis in the 1950s and 1960s, black professionals were not generally offered employment in private industry. It seemed the only employers willing to hire educated African Americans were the government and schools. At Sumner, I had many teachers who challenged me to do my best, including Mr. Preston Ingram, my future father-in-law, who taught chemistry there for forty years. Mr. Ingram had a Master's Degree in Chemistry from the University of Chicago, and many of the teachers at Sumner had similarly prestigious degrees, or even Ph.D.s. We students received the benefit of having these well-educated professionals as demanding teachers and the school has many notable alumni including Arthur Ashe, Chuck Berry, Grace Bumbry, Dick Gregory, Robert Guillaume, Julius Hunter, Tina Turner and Margaret Bush Wilson.

Preston and Pauline Ingram, son Bryan and Kay

In addition to being a respected educator, Mr. Ingram was also a jokester. When he saw a male student talking with a female student and not paying attention to the lesson, he would chant, "Ro-mance without fi-nance is a nui-sance." One morning he entered the classroom waving a piece of paper and announced that one of the students had received a scholarship to Penn State, and then he said, "Oh, I made a mistake, it is the state pen!" He also took great pleasure in asking if any of the students could give him the chemical formula for sea water. When no one responded, he gleefully stated, "$C H_2 O$!"

Mr. Ingram had a daughter, Kathleen, known as Kay, who was in my class at Sumner. And that is how I met my wife. We did not date in high school but knew each other, as we were temporarily in the same student advisory group. I thought Kay was the prettiest of several pretty girls in that advisory group, all of whom were from good families. I felt that I didn't quite fit in with them but was happy enough to be there. Kay and I only began dating some years later after we were both in the weddings of three other Sumner classmates, Wilatrel (née Freeman) Stockton, Beth Ann (née Carter) Thomas and Flim Thomas.

Beth Ann and Flim Thomas   Dr. Clyde and Wilatrel Stockton

While in high school I decided to become a teacher, in part because of the impact my fifth-grade teacher Mrs. Wigley had on my life. As far as I was concerned, then and now, teachers are true heroes who change lives every day. Teachers mold the minds of our next generation; they start with children who are diamonds in the rough and turn them into gems of the highest quality. So after graduating from Sumner High in 1962, I attended Harris Teachers College in midtown St. Louis, a historically black public college, now Harris-Stowe State University.

During college I always had a job, usually working 40 hours per week. Those jobs included being a librarian at the St. Louis Public Library, a clerk at the post office, a sheet metal assembler at McDonnell Douglas (now Boeing), a photo processor at Fotomat, an assembly line worker at Chrysler, and a recreation leader for the St. Louis Parks Department. My second year of college, I worked 60 to 72 hours per week at the post office. In post office lingo, it was called "doing twelves" when you worked 12 hours per day, five to six days a week. It was a challenge to go to school and work that many hours. On a couple of occasions, I was so tired in class that I fell out of my desk to the floor, sound asleep, bringing uproarious laughter from my classmates.

The only job I was ever fired from was at McDonnell Douglas, the summer after my first year in college. They hired me as a sheet metal assembler, despite the fact that my mechanical skills were nonexistent and the job required those skills and more. I was poorly qualified but extremely proud of that good-paying job; I liked wearing the McDonnell Douglas badge on my shirt and had no intention of returning to school. They fired me two weeks after college resumed from summer break, after I did a poor job of riveting a fuel dump into the wing of a plane and it had to be redone by a journeyman assembler. Thank goodness I was allowed to re-enroll late at Harris. God had other plans for me!

In 1966, I graduated from Harris and got a job teaching fifth graders at Cote Brilliante Elementary School in St. Louis, where I had briefly attended school as a child. While teaching, I was also working another 40 hours per week on the side as a recreation leader for the City. I taught for two years at Cote Brilliante, but quickly realized that as much as I admire teachers, I was not cut out to be a teacher. Teaching is a very hard job requiring tremendous patience, which is not my forte. After the first year of teaching, I enrolled in a Master of Business Administration program at the University of Missouri at Columbia (Mizzou), thinking that I would find out what I wanted to do. While teaching, I took basic business courses at night at the University of Missouri at St. Louis and transferred the credits to Mizzou, and spent summers in Columbia taking courses at Mizzou.

During the years I was in college and graduate school, our country was going through turbulent times. Across the nation, African Americans were standing up for equal rights. Progressive whites did join in the protests, but all too often small-minded people responded with violence. On April 4, 1968, Martin Luther King, Jr. was assassinated. I was working at the library when I heard the news and was quite distraught. It was not comforting when the security guard commented to me that Dr. King was a communist. Feeling dispirited, I did not go to work the next day, and the day after that I drove to Washington, D.C. to visit Kay. Following Dr. King's death, civil disorder and race riots were happening in many cities across the country, and D.C. was one of the most severely affected. Columbia Heights was an African-American commercial center in D.C., the heart of which was located at Fourteenth and U Streets Northwest. Kay had recently moved to a new apartment in Columbia Heights, two blocks west at Sixteenth and U Streets. She was too close to the riots for comfort.

I wasn't that familiar with D.C., and as I got closer to Columbia Heights many streets were barricaded. It was almost surreal to see barbed wire, tanks and young National Guard soldiers patrolling the streets with assault rifles, probably AK-47s. Kay's building was hard to get to on a normal day, as her portion of the street was only a block long and was closed off on both ends. With so many of the streets being blocked by barbed wire or tanks, I ran into numerous dead ends and could not figure out how to get to her place. There were no cell phones in those days of course, and I certainly wasn't going to get out of my car to find a payphone, so I reluctantly concluded I had to stop and ask the soldiers for directions. I was nervous at first, but the soldiers were friendly to me and as helpful as possible, but they also were not familiar with D.C. I ended up having several conversations with National Guard soldiers before I finally arrived at Kay's. All the while, smoke was billowing from the downtown D.C. area. I was very relieved to finally arrive. Seeing this made me realize that in the shadows of the white marble buildings in D.C. sat a tinderbox. I did not sense that the African Americans in St. Louis had this same outward rage about race.

Law School

In 1969, Kay and I were married and I moved to D.C. where she was working as a school teacher. I got a job teaching fifth grade at Harriet Tubman Elementary School, and continued taking courses toward my M.B.A. at the University of Maryland and George Washington University, and was able to transfer course credits back to Mizzou.

One of the classes I took while living and teaching in D.C. was an elective business law class at the University of Maryland taught by Professor Gary Mazza. I knew nothing about the law, lawyers or judges.

Becoming a lawyer only entered my mind after taking this class. The Socratic method of instruction took hold of me and that proverbial light bulb came on. I realized, *This is what I want to do*! I was genuinely enamored with the case law method and the logic involved, and decided that law school would be my next step.

I wanted to finish my M.B.A. degree, so I attended Mizzou full time from January 1971 through August 1971 to complete it. Because Kay enjoyed her teaching job in D.C., I applied to several law schools there, including American University, Howard University, George Washington University and The Catholic University of America. In the spring of 1971, an African-American law student from Catholic University, Lawrence M. (Larry) Lawson, now a judge in Montclair, New Jersey, visited me in Columbia, Missouri, I assume as part of an outreach program to prospective African-American students. Larry convinced me that Catholic was a perfect fit for me. Larry said law school would be challenging, but that Catholic had a nurturing environment, and I was very impressed that Catholic University sent him to visit me. In addition, they offered me a full scholarship, while the other schools had offered only partial scholarships.

Larry was right. Law school was a challenge but a very gratifying experience, as I continued to enjoy the logic of the law and the teaching method, and ended up ranking high in my class. I was also gratified because I was able to recruit my brother Booker and his friend Gary Cook to follow me to Catholic University to attend law school.

During my second year of law school, I obtained a clerkship at the National Labor Relations Board (NLRB) through one of my law professors, Roger Hartley, who had been a star attorney at the NLRB before joining the faculty at Catholic University School of Law. I had done well in his labor law class. One of the best things to come out of my NLRB clerkship happened in about 1973. A Howard University law student was also clerking there. He got engaged and I was invited to his bachelor party, where I met his friend Bernard Shaw, who was then a correspondent for CBS News. Bernie and I started talking about the fact that we had the same last name and just hit it off. Although Bernie's family is from Chicago, they have roots in Tennessee where my family is from. We've always assumed we could be distantly related, but never looked into it. Bernie and I became great friends and have stayed so for all these years.

Bernie's friendship has meant a lot to me and we have had many good times together. One highlight was in 1979, after Bernie had moved to ABC News to be its Latin American correspondent and was living in Miami, Florida. Bernie was invited to attend Super Bowl XIII in ABC News president Roone Arledge's seats on the fifty-yard line at the Orange Bowl, but due to other commitments Bernie gave the seats to Kay and me. I'm not the biggest football fan, but we went and were fortunate to witness the Pittsburgh Steelers defeat the Dallas Cowboys 35-31 in a wild game. I'll never forget seeing the famous blunder when former St. Louis Cardinal football and Dallas Hall of Fame tight end Jackie Smith dropped Roger Staubach's potential game-tying pass in the end zone on third down.

I graduated from Catholic University School of Law in 1974 and passed both the Washington, D.C. and Missouri bar exams. George Draper, Sr., an African-American Superior Court judge in D.C., administered the oath of office and swore me in to the Missouri bar. I had appeared before Judge Draper while in law school in a Law Students in Court class. Upon graduation from law school, the NLRB offered me a job in D.C. as an enforcement litigation attorney. I gladly accepted and worked there for two years, primarily writing briefs and arguing cases concerning labor law before the federal courts of appeal throughout the United States.

Booker and I returned home to St. Louis in 1976, after his graduation from Catholic University School of Law. Booker became a prosecutor and I entered private practice. Although we had dreamed of practicing law together, it only came to fruition when we were both state circuit judges in the City of St. Louis. They say dreams do come true, but often not as you foresaw them. That is how it was with us.

CHAPTER TWO

Home Sweet Home

As the car wound through the Appalachian Mountains, my eyes were on the winding highway but my mind was on returning to home sweet home, St. Louis. It had been seven years since my marriage and move to Washington, D.C. in 1969, and I was returning to my roots. Both my brothers were back living with our parents at the old homestead in north city, and I was going to temporarily live with them until my wife Kay returned, as she was finishing out her teaching duties for the school year. We were always a close-knit family and I was anticipating Dad's admonition every time I departed the premises, "Watch everything."

The three sons, the ABC brothers, Alvis Jr., Booker and Charles were living together again as adults, if only for a few months. It was August 1976, and Booker had returned from Washington, D.C. in June after he finished law school, and Alvis was going through a transition (a trial marital separation). We brothers knew the drill, and after a taste of freedom, being back under our parents' roof again would be a challenge. Mother felt that however well you performed a task there was room for improvement. For Dad, life was a serious enterprise where time for play came only after your assigned task was completed. And he had tasks.

The ABC Brothers

The City of St. Louis was changing. The St. Louis I knew as a child was segregated. All black people lived in the same neighborhoods, went to the same schools and didn't venture far from home. The neighborhood grocery stores were thriving, there was less serious violence than today, as police patrolled their beats and the houses were well kept. Now, in 1976, the black neighborhoods were gradually deteriorating as middle class and more affluent African Americans moved to the county with its perceived better schools and integrated communities. They were seeking a better life for themselves and their children.

My life had sure changed, and I had a sense of great anticipation. I was married; my wife, Kay, was expecting; and now two years out of law school I was joining a well-respected law firm. The law firm of Lashly, Caruthers, Theiss, Rava & Hamel (now Lashly & Baer) had offered me a position as an associate. Booker was working as an Assistant Circuit Attorney for the City of St. Louis under Circuit Attorney George Peach. My feelings were positive and upbeat as Booker and I were provided a great legal education at Catholic University. I was confident that success was inevitable.

Within a few weeks of my return to St. Louis from Washington, D.C. as a lawyer, state Circuit Judge Daniel Tillman (now retired) took me to lunch at the Metropolitan Bar Association. Judge Tillman was a long-time friend and hunting buddy of Dad's. He told me it wasn't that long ago that African Americans could not be members or dine there. Black folks of Judge Tillman and my parents' generation didn't go to restaurants, because they knew they were not welcome there. This mindset carried over to my generation. Dad and his friends would host social events and parties at their houses instead, and all the kids would go, too.

Judge Tillman's statement caused my mind to reflect on the first time I went to a St. Louis restaurant, at age sixteen. It was near Christmas and I had gone downtown on the bus and was hungry from hours of holiday shopping. I approached a Chinese restaurant and was stopped at the door by an Asian gentleman who said, "We do not serve blacks." This was one of my first encounters with open racism when I was old enough to realize what was going on. I thought at the time it was ironic that one minority was discriminating against another. I knew the South was a different situation, but I truly didn't feel personally discriminated against in St. Louis until I was turned away from that restaurant. After this incident at sixteen, I didn't go to another restaurant until I was twenty-four years old and living in D.C.

When I was turned away, my mind then raced to childhood and our yearly summers on Grandmother's farm thirteen miles outside of Jackson, Tennessee. When Mother would leave to return to St. Louis she gave us the drill about going to town on Saturday: "When you go into the drugstore to get a soda or candy, address the white teenage workers as 'Sir' or 'Ma'am,' and do not take a seat. And, of course, only use the 'colored' water fountain and under no circumstances the 'whites' one." We strictly obeyed her directive as Emmett Till's 1955 murder in Mississippi was a heavy mental reminder of the potentially dangerous results of violating the rules of segregation.

During lunch with Judge Tillman, he told me that he would have to "tuffin" me up. He said he needed to take me into an alley and hit me upside the head with a brick. With his size, thank goodness he was only jesting. Judge Tillman merely wanted me to realize that being a lawyer was serious business and the weak may not survive. I got the memo.

Private Practice at the Lashly Firm

Private practice was spent working long hours on cases. Then, as now, law firms expected associates to work a large amount of billable hours. Lashly had a number of high profile clients, including the St. Louis School Board, Bi-State Development, and The Board of Healing Arts. These clients carried great public interest and were frequently in the news. In the mid 1970s the St. Louis school desegregation case (*Liddell v. Board of Education*) was the biggest story around. Like the city itself, St. Louis metropolitan schools were segregated by race. Integration in the city and the county had failed and now the matter was in the hands of the federal courts. The *Liddell* case would decide who would be attending what schools in the St. Louis metropolitan area. There was great anticipation. Lashly represented the St. Louis Public Schools, which sought to have the county schools allow black students to be bused into their school system and to have them pay for it to boot. This was high stakes involving the community's children and its tax dollars.

In late 1977, John Lashly was preparing to argue the *Liddell* case before the Eighth Circuit Court of Appeals. The Friday evening before his Monday morning argument, about twenty-five of the firm's lawyers were gathered in Lashly's lower level lounge peppering John with questions, suggestions and ideas. As the most senior partner and namesake of the firm, John Lashly was well respected and was highly thought of by all. John had visited Catholic University with an American Bar Association accreditation delegation during my last year in law school, and I was his escort for the school tour. At that time, I expressed my interest in returning to St. Louis and practicing with a firm. We hit it off and even discussed the possibility of an associate position for me with his firm, which later came to pass.

John Lashly was always diplomatic and gracious, had the most clients and personally sponsored me for bar membership in the U.S. District Court for the Eastern District of Missouri. John was tall, handsome, and oozed class. He was what you wanted to see in a lawyer of his stature, and that is what I saw and respected.

As the questions and thoughts ebbed and flowed about the school desegregation argument, senior partner Ted Weakley (now deceased) took center stage. He waxed on about the case and detoured to a conversation about Theodore McMillian, the newest judge on the Eighth Circuit Court of Appeals and its first African-American member. Ted stated that perhaps Judge McMillian should not sit on this case as he was a member of the NAACP. I wondered where he was going with this and what he might suggest should be done. After there was no response from the gaggle of associates and partners, Ted took a severe detour, in fact, he made a ninety-degree right turn. Apparently forgetting that I was present, Ted proclaimed that if he were black he would have to be paid thirty million dollars. His proclamation was met with utter silence until I responded, "Aww, Ted, if you were black one Friday night you might have so much fun that you would never want to be white." Again, there was complete silence and our brainstorming session came to an abrupt end. Perhaps my blunt sense of humor, especially on issues of race, was too much for some to handle.

The next day, Saturday morning, Ted stopped by my office and told me he didn't mean anything by his statement. I responded that neither did I. It was never spoken of again by anyone in the firm, at least not in my presence. I accepted the fact that racism existed and some people put a premium on being white, but I felt pleased that I had responded with a great stereotypical retort. Years later, as a federal judge I told this story to a *St. Louis Post-Dispatch* columnist and concluded with the statement, "And I'm still waiting for my thirty million dollars." He didn't laugh either but turned red and abruptly walked out of my office. Even with the passage of time, I've found that my humor can leave some folks speechless.

At the firm I didn't always feel comfortable enough to speak my mind. I remember one incident at the Lashly firm that left me speechless. It was Labor Day 1976, and I had just been at the Lashly firm for a couple of weeks. Even though it was the holiday weekend, in private practice you still went to work. As I approached the elevator I saw Paul Rava, a name partner in the firm, who was dressed in a suit and tie. I had on a polo shirt and khakis and was somewhat alarmed as a new associate. I always wore a suit and tie on weekdays, but this was a Saturday. Naively, I inquired of Paul, "Is everyone else dressed like that today?" Paul responded, "I don't dress below a certain standard." I was thinking that maybe I wasn't meeting his standard. When we got up to the office, everyone else was dressed casually like me. I guess all the attorneys in the firm weren't meeting his standard either.

By the end of 1978, I was working in Lashly's Clayton office and name partner Hap Hamel had taken me under his wing. Hap had banking and business clients with whom I worked. The Clayton office had a very congenial atmosphere and my time in that office was quite relaxed in contrast to the more intense downtown office. When I went back to the main downtown office after two years in Clayton, it was apparent to me that it was time to move on. I felt there was no room for growth and I was not as interested in the work. I wanted to be on the front lines, in the heat of battle, evaluated by my own victories or defeats and not someone's subjective opinion. I set my sights on becoming a federal prosecutor.

Albert Stephan became a judge on the Missouri Court of Appeals while a partner at Lashly. Before his appointment, he and I had become fast friends and would often share a cocktail after work. Photography was my hobby at the time and he trusted me to be the official photographer at his swearing-in ceremony. I was flattered by this. He and another partner, Bill Buckley, were instrumental in my moving on to the U.S. Attorney's Office in 1980. My time at Lashly was one of growth and improvement, and the firm provided many opportunities that I appreciated.

During my years at the Lashly firm, I was fortunate to have associated with John Lashly and Hap Hamel as well as a number of other fine attorneys at the firm, including John Fox Arnold, Ken Brostron, Bill Buckley, Darold Crotzer, Thomas Cummings, Ed Filippine, Nelson Howe, Steve Lambright, Mark Mittleman, Alan Pratzel, Paul Rava, Bill Rutherford, Dalton Schreiber, Richard Schreiber, Albert Stephan, Tom Tueth, Charlie Valier, Rick Watters and Ted Weakley.

U.S. Attorney's Office

The idea of working as an attorney for the United States and prosecuting federal crimes greatly appealed to me at that stage of my life. In 1980, I applied for a position with the U.S. Attorney's Office, supported by the helpful recommendations of Lashly partners Al Stephan and Bill Buckley, who had good relationships with Robert D. Kingsland, Sr., the U.S. Attorney for the Eastern District of Missouri. Kingsland and U.S. District Judge Edward Filippine (now retired) had benefitted greatly from their work and association with U.S. Senator Thomas F. Eagleton. After he retired from the Senate, Eagleton was perhaps the most famous practicing attorney in the state. He and former St. Louis Circuit Attorney Edward L. Dowd, Sr. were the first public officials in the area to hire African-American attorneys. After my first year in law school, I had temporarily clerked for Senator Eagleton in his Washington D.C. office.

Tom Eagleton and Ed Dowd, Sr.

My interview went well and I was hired as an Assistant United States Attorney. I was thrilled to be in the U.S. Attorney's Office. It offered opportunities I didn't have in private practice. Once more I was back in court. *Bro rabbit was in the briar patch again.* While at the NLRB I had written briefs and argued cases before a number of the nation's federal courts of appeal. Now I was in the trial court and doing hand-to-hand combat. The heat of battle was exhilarating and I grew very comfortable in the courtroom. When necessary, I would write briefs and argue cases before the Eighth Circuit Court of Appeals. The rush of trial battle was instant adrenalin, while the appellate argument was a contest of wits. It seemed to be the perfect job.

The U.S. Attorney's Office had eighteen or nineteen lawyers and everyone handled all kinds of cases. There were bank robberies, government and bank frauds, large-scale drug distribution cases, firearm cases and others. There were no sentencing guidelines and the judge's only limitation at sentencing was the maximum allowed by the violated statute and the arguments of counsel. It did not seem that the sentences were severe or harsh, just fair. Unlike today, there were no guidelines that punished a defendant exercising his Sixth Amendment right to trial by jury, or enhanced a defendant's sentence for exercising the right to testify in his own defense.

As U.S. Attorney, Bob Kingsland had few rules and accorded all the AUSAs in his office significant independence. He said there was only one star in the office and that was him, but he was loyal to his staff. Kingsland made sure we received all available salary increases and allowed us to attend one legal conference per year at government expense. This was good for morale, including mine.

Evelyn Baker, who had previously been a trial attorney in the City Circuit Attorney's Office as well as the St. Louis County Prosecuting Attorney's Office, was at the time the lead black Assistant U.S. Attorney. Larry Hale was the only other brother AUSA. Evelyn looked after Larry and me like a mother hen. We were the three African Americans on the staff of federal prosecutors. We called ourselves "The Three Musketeers," but the whole staff was a tight group. We partied after every victory as well as the occasional loss. At the time, it was the best job I had ever experienced.

Evelyn Baker, Judge and former AUSA

There was always a lot of good-natured joking in the office and many elaborate practical jokes were played. Tim Wilson, now a Missouri circuit judge, was known as a particularly dedicated and creative practical joker. Many of Tim's best efforts from those days can't be publicly discussed even now, and he continued to play pranks on me after we both became state judges. Tim and others in the office loved to joke with first assistant AUSA Terry Adelman, who is a U.S. Magistrate Judge, about his being from East St. Louis, Illinois, and often claimed that for Terry, a pigeon was a chicken. One day, Tim put a bag of birdseed on Terry's desk with a large hole carefully cut in the bottom. When Terry saw the birdseed sitting on his desk he was upset and grabbed the bag, scattering seed all over his desk and onto the floor, exactly what Tim had anticipated.

In 1981, Thomas E. Dittmeier was named U.S. Attorney, replacing Kingsland. On the credenza behind his desk, Tom Dittmeier proudly displayed a large bust of John Wayne wearing a cowboy hat. One day the bust disappeared. Dittmeier was clearly upset, to say the least, but the bust remained missing and the office was rife with speculation about what had happened to it. Finally, Dittmeier sent out a memo asking that the bust be returned and promising that if it was, nothing more would be said. A week or so later, the bust quietly reappeared in its place of prominence in Dittmeier's office. No one ever admitted to the kidnapping of the John Wayne bust. There is no proof, but in my heart I believe Tim Wilson's fingerprints were all over that one.

Sometimes the source of the jokes and banter came from the courtroom. AUSA Mitch Stevens, who handled many tax and financial institution fraud cases, once asked me to handle a sentencing hearing in a fraud case for him in which the defendant had pleaded guilty and was awaiting sentencing. I appeared in the courtroom before Judge Filippine for the sentencing hearing and was surprised to see that the defendant was a beautiful blonde woman who, strangely, had really big feet. Judge Filippine almost appeared to be on the verge of tears as he sentenced this lovely creature to jail time. Reporting later to Mitch about how the sentencing had gone, I remarked that the judge seemed to think it was terrible this beautiful woman had to go to jail. I also mentioned the woman's large feet, which had stuck in my mind. Mitch laughed uproariously and said, "Didn't you notice her large Adam's apple as well?" The beautiful woman was actually a man and Mitch, who later became a federal administrative law judge and is now in private practice, teased me about her for years after that.

AUSAs were often sent to retreats and seminars to learn new strategies and procedures and to hone our skills. During one retreat at the Lake of the Ozarks in south-central Missouri, a number of us went to a restaurant for dinner. Shortly after we were seated, we heard a large group at the table adjacent to us using the N-word. We looked at each other in disbelief, and Larry Hale pointed it out to the rest of our group. Ed Dowd, Jr. immediately sprang from his seat with Mike Reap and Larry Hale right behind him. Ed forcefully confronted each individual at the table of a dozen or so people, repeatedly inquiring, "Did you say that?" and looking as if he was ready to fight. Each person said "no," and the final individual, a man who probably weighed three hundred pounds, said, "No, and it's over." Their group then promptly departed the restaurant. Although the confrontation was over, it told all of us, especially Evelyn Baker, Larry Hale and me, where Ed and Mike stood as far as matters of race were concerned. The AUSAs in the office were a tight group and this incident exemplified it. Although we had fun, we were very serious about our work and fair play.

The other AUSAs were always willing to help if complications arose with a case. Dick Poehling, Evelyn Baker and I all had criminal trials set before Judge William L. Hungate in April 1983. Judge Hungate would set all of his cases, civil and criminal, for trial on the first Monday of the month. There might be a dozen or more cases set for the same day, so it could take most of the month for all of the cases to be tried. My wife Kay had been fortunate enough to have a business trip to Hawaii scheduled in early April, and we decided I would go along and take advantage of the opportunity to have a vacation. Unfortunately, the trip conflicted with the trial date. Dick and Evelyn readily agreed to try their cases first and second on Judge Hungate's April docket, so I could go to Hawaii and return in time to try my case third. The three of us appeared before Judge Hungate in March and proposed this solution.

Judge Hungate had a commanding and authoritative style, as he had been a U.S. Congressman before becoming a federal judge. As a member of the House Judiciary Committee, he sponsored the second of three articles of impeachment against President Richard Nixon during the Watergate proceeding. Judge Hungate rejected our proposal out of hand and said with complete seriousness, "Mr. Shaw, I suggest you take your vacation when I take mine, in August." To say that Kay and I were disappointed would be an understatement, and my coworkers knew it. A couple of weeks later, the defendant in my case was shot in the leg and the trial date had to be continued to a later time. People in the U.S. Attorney's Office teased me mercilessly, saying, "Charles, you didn't have to shoot him!"

Kay and I did get to take that trip and had a wonderful time. I had taken up golf not long before and was not a good golfer at all, but wanted to play a round at the Princeville Resort on Kauai, which was on a list of the 100 greatest golf courses. I rented a cart and took Kay out with me on the course. Kay doesn't golf and she sat in the cart reading a book, but would look up occasionally from her book to watch me hack away. Not impressed, she asked, "You can't hit the ball any better than that?"

Later, she said, "You keep hitting those balls in the ocean and pulling out another one and dropping it. How much do those balls cost?!"

The late Judge Kenneth Wangelin was my favorite judge when I was an AUSA. He was down to earth, plain spoken, well liked and was quite a character. He kept a .38 pistol in his desk and would take it out of his desk and twirl it around his finger as he told jokes and stories. Back in that day, federal district judges had what was called "informal matters" two to three mornings a week. These half-hour sessions provided lawyers the opportunity to make walk-in appearances for short, simple matters such as continuances or to advise the court of a game-changing development in their case. Judge Wangelin always started his session by asking, "Does the government have any informal matters?" The AUSAs would present their issues and private counsel would follow. In other courtrooms, there was no such preference given to the government and the AUSAs. It was just informal matters and whoever approached the podium first was heard. Generally, the AUSAs allowed private counsel to precede them and all went smoothly.

One morning I needed to be in two courtrooms for informal matters. I intended to be first to the podium, get my matter before the judge, and move on to the other courtroom before the half-hour informal matters period ended. The first courtroom was that of Judge Edward Filippine, who had been at the Lashly firm before going to the federal bench. I got to Judge Filippine's courtroom early and positioned myself to be the first to the podium. Judge Filippine looked me in the eye and stated, "We'll take the government's matters last!" I was nonplussed, belittled and somewhat embarrassed in the lawyer-filled courtroom, and concerned as to whether I could get to the next courtroom timely. It all worked out but I never forgot that occasion. When I became a member of this same federal bench, I was one of the last judges to continue the tradition of informal matters. In deference to the AUSAs, who are often scrambling, I started my informal matters with the question, "Does the government have any informal matters?"

Another tidbit I picked up from Judge Wangelin was how he ended the first day of trial with the admonition to the jury. As I've mentioned, in 1976 when I returned home from Washington, D.C., I initially resided with my parents. Mother was Mrs. Law and Order, not tolerating any detour or frolic from the designated path. One week she was on jury duty in federal court and as a young novice lawyer I was quite interested. So I asked her if she had been selected to serve on a case and she said, "Yes." Then I asked, "What kind of case is it?" She forcefully responded, "The judge told me not to discuss that with you!" Case closed.

About seven years later I was trying a case in Judge Wangelin's courtroom. At the end of the first day he gave the jury the formal admonition not to discuss the case with anyone and then stated, "Let me simplify this for you. When you go home your friends and family will know that you have been down here for jury service. So, the first question they will ask you is whether you were selected to serve on a case. The answer is 'Yes!' The next question will be, 'Well, what kind of case is it?' The answer is, 'The judge told me not to discuss that with you!'" This statement brought back the memory of seven years before and made me realize how true his statement was and how simple it made the admonition. This was another gem for me to use later when I became a trial judge. Thank you, Judge Wangelin.

Another notable judge during my time as an AUSA was Judge John Nangle. Judge Nangle was universally thought to be the sharpest judge in the federal courthouse. We called him the "Silver Fox." He had beautiful silver hair and could outfox the brightest of them all. Judge Nangle's intellect was inspiring. He was the Chief Judge, but his office was always open for advice and guidance. He was helpful in my becoming a state judge.

I tried many cases as a federal prosecutor. The only trial I lost while in the U.S. Attorney's Office was against the late, well-known attorney Charles M. Shaw. They say you learn more from your losses than your wins, and I don't disagree. I later realized I made a mistake during jury selection by leaving a retired military lawyer on the jury. I had served on a jury myself two years after graduating from Harris-Stowe in 1968, and realized from the experience that jurors are looking for someone to lead them. I assumed a retired military lawyer would be a natural leader and more inclined to favor the government's case, but in this particular instance I was wrong. Sometime after the trial, I became aware that Charlie Shaw had been a prisoner of war during World War II who escaped, and that Steve McQueen's character in the movie *The Great Escape* was based on him. Not only was he a great lawyer, but a war hero to boot. Charlie won that case in jury selection before any evidence was presented. Lesson: Know your adversary's history and never leave anyone of leadership quality on the jury panel unless you are absolutely positive that they will find in favor of your client.

Charles M. Shaw, Criminal Defense Attorney

Charlie M. Shaw was the best criminal defense lawyer in St. Louis. He was truly a legend in his own time. He dominated a courtroom and captivated juries with his booming baritone voice. His jury selection techniques, cross-examination of witnesses and trial tactics were unmatched. At that time, he was the only defense lawyer who would remember all the names and some personal information about each juror on the panel, generally forty or more individuals. During his jury selection questioning, the jurors paid close attention as Charlie might suddenly call on them by name and mention a personal detail. He kept them in a spellbound state as they absorbed his point of view as to whether they were suitable to serve on a case. He strutted around the courtroom and courthouse like he owned it. Charlie drove up to the courthouse in his red Ferrari, wearing a large homburg hat while smoking a big Churchill cigar. He was a showman extraordinaire.

During our trial, in the jury's presence, Charlie protested that a document was improperly disallowed from being admitted into evidence, and dramatically waved it about. He contended that this document should be admissible as it favored his client. I objected to his protestation and when we approached the bench I grabbed the document from his hands. It was blank! At times when we would approach the bench out of the jury's hearing, he would continue to send a message to the jury. Charlie would, while addressing the judge, abruptly turn his head to an unfavorable witness on the stand and waggle his finger toward the witness suggesting that the witness was untruthful. Occasionally, while at the bench he would also waggle his finger at me, suggesting to the jury that I was engaging in some nefarious conduct. Everything Charlie did in the courtroom was designed to turn the jury in favor of his client.

At our trial, the primary government witness against Charlie's client was a Confidential Informant (CI) of the Drug Enforcement Administration (DEA). During cross examination of the CI, Charlie challenged the CI's identification of his client as the perpetrator of the crime. He asked the CI about the perpetrator's height, as compared to his own. Charlie had the CI step down from the witness stand and stood toe to toe with him, asking if he was sure that the person was Charlie's height or taller or shorter. It was a confrontational face off, as if he was about to punch the CI. This was extremely effective in challenging the CI's credibility and demonstrating to the jury that they should not be afraid to question this identification testimony.

The government's case was weak, but I thought we had a good chance of winning. Wrong. After the jury's not-guilty verdict, the case agent suggested that perhaps I should have forgone its prosecution. I must admit I was somewhat influenced by the fact that the case was against my namesake, the best in town, and it was an opportunity for a win against him and, if nothing else, a chance to learn. Boy, was I wrong about the win, but right as to the learning experience.

Thereafter, Charlie and I became quite comfortable in each other's company. When he came to the U.S. Attorney's Office he would ask the receptionist if his son was in, referring to me. I first met U.S. Senator John Danforth when Charlie introduced me to him as his son, and at the same public function he introduced my wife, Kay, as his wife. He was a character and took great pleasure in those introductions. Shaw Park in Clayton, Missouri is named after his father who just happened to have the same name as me, Charles A. Shaw. Charlie M. Shaw died in 2001 and his memorial service was on the morning of 9/11. Many of the area judges and lawyers were in attendance as the events of that terrible day unfolded.

The fact that Charlie Shaw and I had similar names and were both lawyers caused a surprising amount of confusion for the public, despite our different ages and races. Over the years, many people have called my office asking for Charlie Shaw. When my staff told them they had the wrong Charles Shaw, that I was Charles A. Shaw but they wanted Charles M. Shaw, the callers would often insist I had handled their case some years back and say they needed my help again. It was sometimes difficult to make the caller believe he or she had the wrong person. In those instances, my staff would finally resort to asking if the Charlie Shaw the caller knew was a white man or a black man. The answer was always a white man. Those calls continue to come to this day, more than twelve years after Charlie passed away. Charlie was a once-in-a-lifetime lawyer.

Early in my tenure at the U.S. Attorney's Office, fellow AUSA Dick Poehling praised my suit, a brown checkered polyester model. I thanked Dick and proudly stated, "It only cost fifty dollars." Henry "Buzz" Fredericks, another AUSA who was not only a highly respected trial attorney but a sharp dresser as well, was standing with us. Buzz thoroughly eyeballed the suit and promptly proclaimed, "And it looks like it, too!" That suit was never worn again and quickly found its way to Goodwill. After that, my uniform was a dark blue suit, white shirt, repp tie, and the always-present American flag lapel pin, a sharp contrast to the less conservative and more style-conscious suits and ties I like to wear today.

Entirely apart from my colleagues' ribbing, I began to give more consideration to my work attire because it made an impression on others, and I'm not just referring to my co-workers or to jurors in the courtroom. It was apparent that the African-American custodial staff was proud to see black AUSAs, because AUSAs were the next closest thing to the judges in terms of respect they were accorded. The custodians were proud to see black people who had risen to that level. My attire needed to be worthy of my position, and of those who saw black professional progress in me.

Even so, there was another occasion as an AUSA when I was made to feel underdressed. The U.S. Attorney's Office staff would frequently go from our offices on the fourth floor to Bessie's Sandwich Shop on the first floor. Like all the other attorneys and staff, I left my jacket in the office when I went to the sandwich shop. One day in 1982, I caught the elevator going to Bessie's, sans jacket. When the elevator opened on the first floor, there stood Paul Rava, the partner from Lashly who had criticized my Saturday workplace attire years before. He looked me up and down and said in a disparaging tone, "I see you're getting comfortable here." Although I didn't respond to his comment, it made a definite impression on me as I had plans to move on someday. I never left that office again without a jacket as I did not wish to downplay my higher aspirations.

My time as an AUSA was enjoyable and often exhilarating, but after five years I was anxious to move on. I had become the only African-American attorney in the office, as Evelyn Baker had become a state trial judge and Larry Hale had opened his own practice. I was the last of "The Three Musketeers" and decided to focus on becoming a state court judge.

Some of the AUSAs I had the pleasure of associating and working with during my tenure were Judge Terry Adelman, Ed Brzezinski, Judge Rick Buckles, Pam Bucy, Dave Capes, Ben Clark, Judge Kathy Crane, Jim Crowe, Fred Dana, Ed Dowd, Jr., Mike Fagan, Buzz Fredericks, Bob Haar, Debbie Herzog, Steve Higgins, Jim Martin, Joe Moore, Kevin O'Malley, Dick Poehling, Mike Reap, Dave Rosen, Jim Steitz, Mitch Stevens, and Judge Tim Wilson. I am thankful for the memories. It was a great time, in a great office, with great people.

Chapter Three

From Federal Prosecutor to State Judge

Becoming a Missouri state court judge in St. Louis requires getting the judicial selection commission to place your name among the three names sent to the governor, for his selection of one person to become a judge. First you apply to the commission in hopes of becoming one of the three persons selected. This involves interviews, three letters of recommendation, and tons of support by way of calls and letters. The judicial selection commission is chaired by the chief judge of the Missouri Court of Appeals, with two attorney members voted in by fellow lawyers and two lay members appointed by the governor. The commission members individually interview the applicants and subsequently decide on the three to be sent to the governor for his pick.

A number of lawyers applying for the state bench become frustrated after a few unsuccessful applications. After I became a state judge, several discouraged lawyers spoke to me asking for advice. My response was that perseverance is the key. In fact, it was my forte as it took me twelve applications to be appointed to the city circuit court bench.

The first time I applied for a judgeship was for a position on the Missouri Court of Appeals Eastern District, and I made the panel of three lawyers whose names were sent to the governor for decision. My hopes were high. Although I was not selected, making the panel was encouraging. It was 1982 and I had been an AUSA for two years. I applied for the appellate bench because at that time, my heart was still in writing. Prior to returning to St. Louis, ninety percent of my work with the National Labor Relations Board had been research and writing. It was my comfort zone, and I had yet to fully transition to the thrill of trial work. In 1982, before I had many trials under my belt, I thought I would be more qualified as an appellate rather than a trial judge.

After a couple more tries for the state court of appeals, I changed my focus to the trial bench. They say if you shoot for the moon and miss, you might be a star. That was my plan. Besides, after this time, I had achieved a great level of competence and comfort in the courtroom after trying numerous cases as an AUSA against very good lawyers. My role model was former AUSA Evelyn Baker, who left to join the St. Louis city circuit bench.

In 1986, I finally made another judicial panel and I was in the mix for selection by Governor John Ashcroft to the circuit bench. This panel consisted of Associate Circuit Judge Michael Calvin, Robert H. Dierker, Jr. and me. It wasn't long before Dierker was selected, but I was not dismayed. My time came one year later, in the spring of 1987.

At the time, Kay and I were in Hilton Head, South Carolina with our good friends, the late Dr. Clyde Stockton and his wife Wilatrel, our Sumner High School classmate and Kay's godsister. We were their guests at a dental convention. We had driven the many hours there, with a one-night stop over midway. I was in constant contact with supporters in St. Louis as my application for the circuit bench was in play. When the call came from Booker that my name was among the three going to Governor Ashcroft, I hastily drove sixteen hours home to campaign for my selection.

I urged politicians (both Democrats and Republicans), clergy, public officials, associates, friends and family to write and call Governor Ashcroft's office in support of my judicial appointment. The other two lawyers on the panel were Richard D. Schreiber and Timothy G. Noble. My significant opponent was thought to be Schreiber as his father, Dalton, had Republican credentials and Governor Ashcroft was a Republican. In contrast, I had no real political history.

Richard and his father were partners in the Lashly firm while I was there as an associate. Richard was the office manager of Lashly's Clayton office between 1978 and 1979 when I worked there. I remember one day, Richard walked into my office with a check. He was smiling when he handed it to me, and pointed out that the check had been made out to "Charles Black." A day or so prior, a white gentleman who had come to me for a consultation, apparently gave the receptionist the check for my services. While Richard stood at my desk, I turned the check over and endorsed it "Charles Black" and beneath that "Charles Shaw," returned it to him, and went back to work on the document on my desk. Richard was speechless. I was familiar with the legalities of endorsements.

Among the people who supported me in my quest for the state bench was Paul DeGregoria, Director of Elections for St. Louis County, a well-respected Republican. He and his friends gave me suggestions and encouragement. So did federal judges John F. Nangle and Stephen N. Limbaugh, Sr., both Republicans. Among Paul DeGregoria's friends was Al Rotskoff, whose involvement turned out to be crucial. Although my campaigning seemed to be going well, time was fleeting and two of my prominent African-American Republican supporters, James Buford, President of the Urban League of Metropolitan St. Louis, and attorney Jerry Hunter, State Director of Labor Relations, advised me that Governor Ashcroft would not appoint me without the endorsement of my boss, U.S. Attorney Tom Dittmeier. I had tried to get Dittmeier to make that call but it had yet to happen.

One evening, Al Rotskoff called me and said that an attorney was telling people on the St. Louis County Council that Dittmeier was supporting me for the judgeship because I was a bum attorney and Dittmeier wanted me out of the U.S. Attorney's Office. The next morning, I told Dittmeier about this story, and he said he would check it out. Tom Dittmeier had been a Golden Gloves boxer. He loved a fair fight and didn't want anyone misrepresenting him. Several days later, Dittmeier told me that Al Rotskoff's report was true and he soon called Governor Ashcroft on my behalf. Not long thereafter, Ashcroft appointed me to the circuit court for the City of St. Louis. Thank God, I was lucky.

With Kay, Bryan and Governor Ashcroft as he signs my Commission

Wearing the Robe as a State Judge

On July 10, 1987, I was officially sworn in as a judge for the Missouri Twenty-Second Judicial Circuit in the City of St. Louis by Judge Daniel Tillman. I was elated, and became engrossed in doing the best job possible.

Judge Tillman swearing me in as state judge

I remember hearing a police officer say that the first time he put on his uniform, he felt like he was wearing a costume. I had a similar feeling the first time I put on my judicial robe. I felt awkward, like I didn't belong in it. It made me think about a time when I had gotten some new golf shoes that were kind of flashy, and I asked my playing partner, Rick Robbins, if the shoes were just too much. He responded, "Well, play up into them." I knew I would have to "play up into" the judicial role in order to feel comfortable in the robe, so I did.

My first assignment as a judge was to a civil trial division. The master docket system was used in the city. Under it, when a case was ready for trial and a courtroom was available, the case was assigned to that courtroom and that judge. For the judge, this meant quick thinking and catching up on the case and the applicable law. It was immediately apparent that the lawyers on a particular case knew more about their case and the applicable law than I did, and they bore listening to. They had been living and working the case for a couple of years and I had just got the file the morning of trial. Accordingly, I would meet with the counsel for about a half an hour, send for the appropriate number of prospective jurors, review any briefs filed in the case, and hit the law books and relevant cases before starting the trial. It was a rush not only in preparation but in the fast pace of the action.

The master docket system was just the opposite of the individualized docket system employed in the federal district court. In the federal system an individual judge usually has a case from the time it is filed until it is concluded. This gives the judge significant lead time in becoming familiar with the case, the attorneys involved and the relevant law. In contrast, the master docket system in the city prepared me to become a quick study and a referee that is required in a trial. As a referee, a trial judge is largely calling balls and strikes. Those calls are made based on the rules of evidence which are basically the same in federal and state court. Prior to joining the bench, as a trial attorney I was not fond of judges who could not make a reasonably prompt decision on evidentiary issues. In the heat of trial, making timely calls gives the attorneys direction, keeps the case proceeding to a conclusion, and puts the case in the hands of the jury sooner. Just like referees in a sporting event, some judges are better than others. In conversations with lawyers and new judges, I have compared making evidentiary calls to a basketball, football or baseball game and asked: "How can the game proceed if the ref can't make the call?" It would be interminable. I thought about one judge the lawyers nicknamed "the Flipper." Cases in his court took longer to try as he flip-flopped, being indecisive. I swore that would not be me.

In the courtroom, I have the "Lee Trevino Rule." Although we have extensive rules in the federal district court for lawyers' conduct and procedures in each judge's courtroom, I ask attorneys appearing before me for the first time if they are familiar with my major rule, the Lee Trevino Rule. If they say no, I tell them the rule: "As you may be aware, Lee Trevino was a great professional golfer. While playing with an amateur, the amateur asked, 'Lee, how should I hit this ball?' Lee responded, 'Miss it quick!'" I am advising the attorneys that they should be prompt, concise and to the point in their presentations.

For me, the most difficult aspect of being a judge is sentencing defendants. During my second year on the state bench I was assigned to a bulk criminal division. In bulk, I mostly took guilty pleas and sentenced criminal defendants. That year I must have sentenced several hundred individuals. It took a while for me to come to grips with what I was doing. Sentencing individuals is one of the most serious responsibilities of a judge. You are taking away a person's freedom, and perhaps taking a husband or wife away from a spouse, a son or daughter away from a parent, and separating a parent from a child. I would anguish over my sentencing decision both before and after the sentence. There were sleepless nights spent questioning myself as to whether I had done the right thing. I soon concluded that with each sentence I had done the best I could and should put it behind me and move on as there were many more to come. How could I be effective with the new cases if I continued to fret over past cases? Ultimately, I tried to do the right thing, made the call, took a deep breath and moved on.

The first case I heard as a state judge was as an observer to Judge Richard J. Mehan, Sr. I was sitting with Judge Mehan on the bench second-chairing the case. I was observing what he did, how he handled the case, and getting the general idea of what it was like to sit as a judge. Dick Mehan was a highly respected judge and was the Missouri State Director of Judicial Education. This was expected to be a learning experience prior to me flying solo. The case involved a nurse who was marketing training films to St. Louis University Hospital. Upon entering the director's office and giving her sales pitch, he advised her that his staff was watching a training film at that very moment. He ushered her into the viewing room where the X-rated, sexually explicit movie *Deep Throat* was being shown. This nurse was suing the hospital for intentional infliction of emotional distress as a result of the director's actions.

As the trial progressed, the plaintiff (the nurse) wanted to show the movie to the jury while the defendant (the hospital) objected. It became clear to me that Judge Mehan was troubled about this development but eventually decided to show the film. Once the movie started playing, I turned and noticed to my surprise that Judge Mehan had left me alone on the bench. It was a bewildering experience as he had left the bench without any warning. What if there was some further objection or other event that required his judgment? Well, it was his case, so I eased out of my chair and left the bench also. He never discussed why he left the bench, but I later learned that he was an extremely devout Catholic and was likely personally offended by a film of this nature.

I've presided over hundreds of cases in my career. The most emotionally gut-wrenching trials occurred in state court. The *Jones* case was tried in 1991 and involved a ten-year-old girl who was severely burned in a kerosene heater fire. The child was only in the courtroom the day her mother testified. Her face looked like a melted, discolored and disfigured mask without ears. Her hands had no fingers and her feet, although covered, were obviously just stubs. Her mother testified about being present when her daughter's facial bandages were first removed. The child saw her image in the hospital room window and asked her mother, "Who is that?" My court reporter, Tammy Young, had young children of her own and was very upset by this mental image and broke into tears. It was painful for everyone to visualize. I promptly took a recess until all could compose themselves. The jury awarded the child twenty-five million dollars, which was the largest verdict in Missouri state court history at the time. The defendant kerosene company moved for a reduction of the verdict or, in the alternative, a mistrial based on my court reporter's tearful outburst. I denied both motions and the case settled on appeal.

The *Isa* trial was in 1992. This case involved the FBI tape-recorded murder by Zein and Maria Isa of their teenage daughter Palestina, who went by the nickname Tina. Zein was a Palestinian of the Islamic faith and his wife, Maria, was a Brazilian of the Catholic faith. The family's rigid cultural traditions became the basis of tension between Tina and her parents. The Isas were distraught that their daughter had become too Americanized, playing on her high school's soccer and tennis teams as well as taking a part-time job at a Wendy's restaurant. There was also a great amount of conflict in the family because Tina was seeing a young black man who was a classmate.

Around that time, Zein Isa came under federal suspicion for espionage as part of the Abu Nidal terrorist network. The FBI obtained federal court approval to install surveillance microphones in the Isas' home and began taping conversations along with tapping their phones. During the time the Isas were under surveillance, Tina was murdered by her parents in the family's home. Unfortunately, no one was listening at the time of Tina's death. The recorded conversations that took place before, during and after the Isas' murder of their daughter were played for the jury.

The Circuit Attorney for the City of St. Louis, Dee Joyce-Hayes, was the lead attorney for the state while attorney Charles M. Shaw led the defense representing Zein. During the trial the attorneys got into heated disagreements and objections. Charlie, always a gamer, was constantly looking for an opportunity to get his opponent off balance and off of her game. Once while they were up at the bench for my ruling on an objection, Charlie vigorously wagged his finger in Dee's face and said, "Young lady, unless you calm down, you won't live to be as old as me." Dee became visibly upset and was about to unleash a torrent of terribles back at Charlie, but I defused the situation. I gently took hold of Charlie's hand, closed down his wagging finger and while holding onto his hand, looked Dee in the face and said, "Ms. Hayes, Charlie told me the same thing several years ago when we faced off in a trial. As you can see, I'm still here."

When the audio tape recording of the murder was played, the sounds of Tina's life being extinguished were horrid. The coroner's testimony described how the stab wounds to her heart and lungs must have been inflicted. Maria would have had her knees over Tina's arms, and was facing her husband, Zein, who sat on Tina's legs while inflicting the fatal thrusts with a large kitchen knife. Hearing the actual words and sounds as Zein inflicted the mortal wounds on his daughter was raw and heart wrenching. Tina's begging for her life, Maria telling her to "shut up," and Zein demanding in Arabic, "Die quickly! Die quickly!" and finally in English, "Die my daughter, die!" You could hear and feel the life draining from Tina as she gasped for breath while the knife plunged through her breastplate and ribs into her heart and lungs. It was emotionally devastating to hear such depravity and suffering.

The jury found both Zein and Maria guilty of capital murder and recommended that I sentence them both to death. In the State of Missouri, the jury's recommendation as to the sentence cannot be increased by the judge but may be decreased. I had initially decided to sentence Zein to death but Maria to life without the possibility of parole. I felt that Zein had been the more culpable of the two, while his wife, I thought, had a lesser role in the killing and had been controlled by her husband. However, during allocution (the defendant's statement to the judge just prior to the pronouncement of the sentence), Maria stated, "We did the right thing." I saw Charlie Shaw's head lower as he gasped in despair. Maria continued, "My daughter was very disrespectful and very rebellious. We should not have to pay with our lives for something she did." I then sentenced them both to death.

Zein was subsequently charged federally with espionage but died in prison. Maria appealed her sentence and it was reduced to life without parole and she remains in prison. Justice was served, but a young life was tragically ended by the very people who should have been protecting it. For me, the trial was also an early glimpse into issues of terrorism and a culture clash that later became such a large part of all of our lives. Reporter Ellen Harris wrote a book about Tina Isa's murder, *Guarding the Secrets: Palestinian Terrorism and a Father's Murder of His Too-American Daughter*.

Security was robust during the *Isa* trial with numerous deputy sheriffs manning the courtroom and a second metal detector at its entrance. Just prior to this time, someone had come into the courthouse threatening to do bodily harm to Judge Michael Calvin, and a defendant, who was on trial in my courtroom for shooting and paralyzing an individual, was found to have a switchblade in his possession. Because the judges walked several blocks from the courthouse to the parking garage, several of us started packing. Judge Tillman, Judge Calvin, my brother Judge Booker Shaw and I bought extra guns and were going to the shooting range on a regular basis. Booker was telling friends that I was carrying three guns: one in a shoulder holster, one in my waistband, and one in my sock. He also claimed that I was in a mode of Robert De Niro in the movie *Taxi Driver*, challenging people, saying, "You talkin' to me? You talkin' to me?!" Of course, he exaggerated my security concerns as I was only carrying two guns during the trial: one in a shoulder holster and one in my waistband. Better safe than sorry, as I was mindful of the comedian Richard Pryor's admonition, "If somebody gets hurt around here, I'm not going to be the last one."

In state court, unlike federal court, murder cases are a regular affair. In 1994, the circuit judge in charge of the criminal division of the St. Louis circuit court told me that of the 228 persons then being held in the old city jail, 145 were awaiting trial for murder. I tried a number of such cases while serving on the state bench. Presiding over a murder case and viewing multiple photos of the victims is not pleasant. In one murder case a woman was accused of shooting her boyfriend to death. The police officer who questioned her upon arrival at the scene testified the woman said that after a heated argument, the boyfriend followed her into the bedroom where she grabbed a rifle from under the bed, shot him twice, then went into the kitchen, sat down, lit a cigarette and declared, "Break time!" It made murder seem to be a casual affair for some defendants, despite its devastating effect on so many other people. After a while as a judge, you become more desensitized to such shocking and gruesome events.

Judge Dan Tillman, Mentor and Friend

Judge Tillman is a retired state court circuit judge and the first lawyer I knew. He was a great mentor to me when I joined the state court bench. He is about six feet four and two hundred and fifty pounds, an imposing figure. His immense presence was very noticeable and possibly intimidating. This was very apparent when he once stood over another circuit judge in one of our meetings and declared that he was opposed to "putting short pants" on our associate circuit judges by not allowing them to vote on court business. I think he did intimidate some judges because that forever ended any discussion about associates not voting, which they are still allowed to do.

Judge Dan, as some called him, loved guns and hunting. He was one of Dad's hunting buddies and no one was happier when Booker and I joined him as state court circuit judges. Dan tried more cases than almost any other judge on the state bench. He prided himself on his work ethic and he truly enjoyed trying cases. Judge Tillman was a contemporary of well-known federal judges Theodore McMillian and Clyde Cahill. He had paid his dues as a lawyer when attorneys of the African-American persuasion were few and far between. Dan came to St. Louis not long after his first court appearance in his home state of North Carolina. He said the judge looked him in the eye and asked, "What can I do for you, boy?" Dan knew that he needed to move on and friends encouraged him to come to St. Louis. Dan was in good stead with African-American politicians and when the time came, he applied for an opening on the state bench and was appointed by Governor Warren Hearnes. His strong will and steadfastness as a judge were inspiring to me.

With Judge Daniel Tillman

One of my most amusing experiences with Dan after I joined the bench occurred when two elderly lawyers stopped by his chambers while we were having lunch. They reminisced about a multi-week trial they had before Judge Tillman years prior. They said that after the first week of trial a juror asked to speak with the judge. The lawyers along with the juror went into Tillman's chambers. The juror advised Judge Tillman that she had spoken with the Lord the night before and He had advised her that she should not sit on the case. Judge Tillman responded, "I spoke with the Lord this morning and He told me you should."

Judge Dan loved to golf and was affectionately called "Mr. Tee" by our fellow golfers. His wife, Dr. Mary Anne Tillman, is a pediatrician and wonderful lady. Dan had more golf clubs than any golf store. He cussed at my brother when Booker joked, "What are Mary Anne and I going to do with all these clubs when you die?" Dan would also keep a tee behind his ear and its disappearance generally coincided with an extraordinarily long fairway shot by "Mr. Tee." (Golfers are not allowed to use a tee in the fairway.)

One day while I was serving as a state judge, Kay was summoned to the city courthouse for jury duty. She urged me to get her out of serving. I replied that everyone who is qualified must do their civic duty, and that jury service was next to voting in its importance. So, on the appointed day, Kay went reluctantly off to jury duty. That same morning I was starting a criminal trial. As the jurors marched in, lo and behold, Kay was among them. As the prosecutor was questioning the jurors about their qualifications, he said to Kay that he noticed she and the judge had the same last name and wanted to know if we were related. She answered, "Yes, he's my husband!" The prosecutor then inquired if that relationship would cause her any problem if she was chosen as a juror on this case. Kay responded, "Yes, it sure would!" Thereupon she promptly picked up a newspaper, held it up to her face and started reading it. I motioned to my courtroom deputy sheriff, Ronnie Hill, to do something to stop this paper-reading behavior. He looked back at me as if to say, "Are you kidding?" I got his message: more trouble at home if I caused her embarrassment in the courtroom.

When we took our luncheon recess, I spoke with Kay and told her that she shouldn't have been reading a newspaper while the court proceedings were still underway. She calmly stated, "I knew I wouldn't be selected after my answers to those questions." When the jurors returned from lunch to complete the questioning for jury selection, Kay was not among them. I asked Ronnie Hill if he knew of her whereabouts. He said, "Sure do, she went down the hall to Judge Tillman's chambers and he got her excused from jury service." When I got home that evening I asked Kay, "Why did you do that?" She answered, "Because you wouldn't do it and I knew who to see!" Tillman enjoyed making me look bad. Only occasionally could I get him back.

Doris Black was one of the best trial lawyers in St. Louis. She had a unique way with jurors that involved audience participation. She would ask the jurors to nod their heads in response to her question if they agreed. Sometimes she would ask them to tap their feet, other times it would be to clap their hands. Doris tried several cases with me as the judge and she took the jurors to church every time. I was told that her father was a Baptist preacher in Dallas, Texas. She came by her manner naturally.

In one case Doris tried before me, she represented an individual charged with murder. Her client took the witness stand and testified that the reason he shot the victim was because, as a short-order cook, he had eaten too many hamburgers. (As they say, truth is stranger than fiction.) As soon as we took a recess I went directly to Judge Tillman's chambers and told him that the State was considering having him testify to rebut this defendant's reasoning, as it was well known that a man of Tillman's size had eaten hundreds of hamburgers, yet had not killed anyone. Tillman cussed me out as I laughed. In the end, the hamburger defense was not successful and the defendant was found guilty of murder.

Assistant Presiding Judge and "Just Us"

During my last year on the state bench I served as the assistant presiding judge in charge of the criminal assignment division. In that capacity I was sending out criminal cases for trial in the various courtrooms and ruling on defendants' pre-trial motions. Under the master docket system, the number of cases that would be disposed of in a given week was unknown, so multitudes of defendants would be waiting in my cavernous courtroom in anticipation of an open trial courtroom to which they would be briskly dispatched. When the defendants arrived at the assigned courtroom, many would plead guilty, eliminate the need for a jury, and open that courtroom for another case. When some of the trial judges were asked how their week went, the response might be, "All singers, no dancers." This meant that all their cases were guilty pleas and no trials were held.

The majority of the defendants awaiting an open courtroom for a criminal trial in my assignment division were African American. They were so numerous that I privately commented to a friend that when I take the bench on a Monday morning, there are so many black people out there I want to ask, "Do white people commit any crimes?" It was really disheartening to see the parade of shackled African-American male defendants chained together as they were marched from the old city jail or workhouse, which is a medium security institution, into the basement of the Municipal Courthouse at 14th and Market Streets. I hated the sight as it looked like a slave chain gang. I reflected on Richard Pryor's joke, "People come to the court house looking for justice, and that's what they find, 'Just us.'"

A Lesson in Eyewitness Identification

In many cases I tried as a state court judge, eyewitness testimony was offered against the defendant. I maintain a healthy sense of skepticism about the accuracy of eyewitness testimony based on my own experiences and what studies have shown. In the courtroom, eyewitness testimony is powerful evidence for a jury, but it should be used with caution because it is often unreliable. The human memory is not a tape recorder and, what is more, it can be corrupted, even unintentionally. In recent years there have been a number of headlines about innocent persons who were fingered by eyewitnesses and convicted, only to be exonerated many years later by DNA evidence. According to the Innocence Project, eyewitness misidentification has played a role in over 75% of the convictions that have been overturned through DNA testing. (This statistic is taken from the Innocent Project report *Reevaluating Lineups: Why Witnesses Make Mistakes and How to Reduce the Chance of a Misidentification*, available online at http://www.innocenceproject. org/docs/Eyewitness_ID_Report.pdf.)

There are several factors that lead to questionable identifications. It is often the case that the circumstances of the crime can make it difficult for a witness to identify a perpetrator. For example, a crime can occur in a matter of seconds, and the lighting is often less than ideal. But more significantly, witnesses of crime often experience a great deal of stress or trauma, and this is particularly heightened if a weapon is involved. The human brain is not designed to record small details in stressful situations; it is in a fight or flight mode. There is also evidence that people have more difficulty identifying persons of a different race.

In addition to circumstantial factors, there are a number of systematic factors that negatively impact the accuracy of eyewitness identification. These arise from how police investigate crime. Witnesses want to be helpful to the investigation and can feel a great deal of pressure to identify a perpetrator. And when people are uncertain about the exact details of what they saw, they may unconsciously fill in the gaps in their memories with inaccurate information. Traditional line-ups and photo arrays can be unduly suggestive, and witnesses may pick up on subtle cues from law enforcement officers, whether these are intentional or not. Added to this is the fact that a witness's faulty memory can be bolstered when an investigative officer makes affirming statements such as, "You did great," or "We thought that was the guy." All of these factors lead to a high number of faulty identifications.

Early in my law career, I had a lesson in misidentification. I experienced firsthand the stress of being the victim of a crime and the pressure to make an eyewitness identification. One night in the fall of 1979, I was carjacked in north St. Louis. I had stopped to pick up some food at a barbecue joint, got back in my car and was getting ready to turn the key in the ignition, when I heard a tapping on the driver's side window. It was a gun in the hands of a man. Within milliseconds there was tapping on the passenger side window, another gun, another man. The first thought that rushed through my mind was of turning the key, backing up and taking off. My second wave of thoughts was: I never realized how close a gun can be to your head when pointed through the glass of your car window, I am driving a convertible Fiat and if I follow my first thoughts, I will end up a sieve and my young son won't have a father. I decided to follow their commands and exit the vehicle with hands raised. Then I heard the ominous words, "Your money or your life!" One of the robbers was calm and holding the gun steady, while the other's gun was shaking in his hands. The ominous words sunk in. I reached into my pants pockets with both hands and realized I only had about four dollars so, at minimum, I was likely to receive a pistol whipping.

With these thoughts I was reluctant to remove my hands from my pockets until one of the robbers exclaimed, "Get your m**** f**** hands out of your pockets!" I quickly complied and dropped the crumpled bills to the ground. When both men dropped down to retrieve the money, I took off running. Usain Bolt had nothing on me in this hundred-yard sprint. While running I heard the shout, "Come back, we want your jacket, too." Needless to say, I didn't stop sprinting for two blocks until I saw a police car at a restaurant. I was so agitated and out of breath that when I tried to relate what happened I was incomprehensible. After I finally managed to relay the events to the police officer, we returned to the scene to find the car gone.

A week or so later the police found my little red Fiat. It had been stripped and vandalized and was an insurance total. Shortly thereafter, the police arrested a suspect and I went to the station to view a lineup. Although one of the men looked strikingly similar to the calm lead robber who spoke the threatening words, and in my heart and mind I felt and thought he was the perpetrator, I declined to identify him because I was not absolutely certain. I realized how easy misidentification can occur. Under the circumstances of the lineup, I felt that I should identify someone because I wanted the crime solved. Yet, I realized that in such an emotional situation, at night with two guns pointed at me, one of them shaking and both looking like cannons, my concentration was not exactly on identification. My experience leads me to keep an open mind about the value and credibility of eyewitness testimony in similar circumstances.

CHAPTER FOUR

Applying for the Federal Bench, or Close But No Cigar

My tenure on the state circuit bench was both exciting and rewarding, but after some years I began to long to be back in the federal system, as that was where I had my first couple years of practice and subsequently seven years in the U.S. Attorney's Office. The old federal courthouse at Tucker and Market Streets was also the U.S. Customs House where Dad had worked as a U.S. Customs Inspector and I had visited numerous times as a child. I felt it was my destiny to return to work in that building. Although some attorneys viewed those who practiced law in the federal courts as having "federalitis," i.e., they acted superior and omniscient, I saw it as an institution of the highest quality, the place where the best of the best had occasion to be on stage. I yearned to be on that stage again.

In 1991, Michael Williams, publisher and editor of the *St. Louis Sentinel* newspapers, urged me to seek a position on the federal bench. Mike was a member of U.S. Senator John Danforth's judicial commission, whose responsibility was to name a group of three candidates from which Senator Danforth would select a candidate for the federal bench and forward that name to the President. At first, I rebuffed Mike's urging that I apply, but he was not deterred. While I was out of town, Mike talked to Kay, and explained why it was to my benefit to seek the position. When I got home, there was an earful waiting for me and I eventually capitulated, despite my desire to wait for a future opening. My former boss, U.S. Attorney Tom Dittmeier, was applying, and my plan had been to help him through. But Mike wanted me. He said that he needed my help in having a well qualified African-American applicant, and that applicant was me. I considered that Mike was a long-time, well-respected friend, a Sumner High School classmate of both Kay and me, and there was no point in creating tension in my relationship with him, as well as with my wife. Besides, Mike might be a federal judicial commissioner in the future and getting on the federal bench was my eventual goal. Furthermore, a happy wife makes for a happy life. As President Bill Clinton said, "Your life is shaped by the opportunities you turn down as well as by those you seize."

Michael Williams

I submitted my application, interviewed with the commission, and made the panel. It was uplifting, and I immediately called Booker and Mike Calvin, both of whom were fellow judges on the circuit bench. We decided to share a cocktail after work that day to celebrate. Before that time arrived, however, Senator Danforth called and gave me the news that Missouri Court of Appeals Judge Jean C. Hamilton was the pick. I promptly called Booker and Mike to cancel the celebration, but they declared, "We can still stop off for a cocktail, but we will just pass a drink under your nose." I got absolutely no sympathy from those guys, just chuckles as if, "You should have known." Nevertheless, I had honored

Mike Williams' request and felt I was in a good position for subsequent openings.

With Michael Calvin and Booker

Getting on the Federal Bench, and Those Who Helped Pull Up My Bootstraps

The late George Smith was one of the most significant people, along with Judge Michael Calvin, the late Judge Theodore McMillian of the Eighth Circuit Court of Appeals, and Betty Jean Kerr (founder, long-time CEO and namesake of the Betty Jean Kerr People's Health Centers), who influenced Congressman Bill Clay, Sr. to send my name to President Clinton as a nominee for the federal bench. You may ask, "Who was George Smith?" In life, there are many unsung heroes and for me, he is among them.

George was a friend and confidant of all the St. Louis political powers that were in and around the black community from the 1950s through the 1990s. He never sought power, fame or fortune for himself. George took pleasure in helping others. In 1967, my friend Flim Thomas was driving my 1967 Corvette with me as passenger. (The money I earned teaching and working a second full-time job, combined with living at home with my parents, though I paid rent, allowed me to buy that car.) Flim was speeding in University City and outran the police. When we eventually got back home, Dad said the University City police wanted to see us. Flim and I, along with Dad and George Smith, went to see their police chief. George knew the police chief. The pursuing officer pointed me out as the driver of the speeding vehicle (another personal lesson in misidentification). Flim immediately volunteered that it was him and that he only sped away because he was black, driving a brand new Corvette in a white neighborhood, and became afraid when he saw the police. That was the end of that. From this experience, I learned that George Smith knew people.

George associated with and advised all the black St. Louis political leaders of the day, including Fred Weathers, Jordan Chambers, J.B. "Jet" Banks, Bill Clay, Sr., and a number of others. Mr. Smith's real job was that of a U.S. Customs Inspector, the same as Dad. They were good friends. George Smith's wife was the former Garnette Granberry, twin sister of Wade Granberry, the owner of Wade's Funeral Home, which is a prominent fixture in the black community in St. Louis. The funeral home's "Twin Chapel" was so named in her honor. Garnette owned the Comet Grill located at Sarah Street and Finney Avenue, which was a prime dining spot in the black community. She was highly respected in the St. Louis restaurant industry and served as Vice President of the Missouri Restaurant Association. Alvis and I had worked at the Comet Grill as teenagers, where we learned invaluable lessons in producing a good product, and providing excellent service in a clean and calm environment. George and his wife Garnette were great role models.

George Smith and Garnette Granberry Smith

George Smith was a talented musician and an outstanding trumpet player. He served as president of Musicians Local 2-197 for fifty years and was instrumental in integrating the Saint Louis Symphony Orchestra. He encouraged and influenced Booker in music by taking him to the Local's practice sessions. George Smith helped Bill Clay, Sr. as a young man with a job at a restaurant. Clay never forgot it, and he listened to George's request that Clay send my name to President Clinton as a nominee for the federal bench. Supreme Court Justice Thurgood Marshall once said, "None of us got where we are solely by pulling ourselves up by our bootstraps. We got here because somebody, a parent, a teacher, an Ivy League crony or a few nuns, bent down and helped us pick up our boots." Thank God for George Smith, a good man who played a major role in my becoming a federal judge.

The Confirmation Process, or A Thorough Vetting

After Congressman Clay sent my name to President Clinton on March 16, 1993 for appointment to the federal bench, the confirmation process started. There was an American Bar Association (ABA) investigation and review as well as a separate investigation by the FBI. The ABA investigation obtains information from members of the bar and the courts as to the potential nominee's practice of law, suitability for the bench, and whether they believe the nominee is qualified. The U.S. Department of Justice gave me a multi-page questionnaire that I had to complete for the White House. It asked about family, friends, finances, associates, neighbors, medical history, employment, education, college and law school transcripts, and places of residence for the past twenty years. It also requested written authorization for federal investigators to obtain information from any of these sources as well as numerous others.

Several friends, neighbors and relatives advised me that the FBI had interviewed them about me. Cousin Edison Mosley likes to take credit for my confirmation based on his positive comments to the FBI. After I passed muster with the ABA and FBI, the Senate Judiciary Committee sent me another questionnaire. It asked for the same information but also asked about my judicial philosophy. Eleanor Dean Acheson, Assistant to the Attorney General, assigned a Deputy Assistant Attorney General (DAAG) to help me with any questions or problems that arose. He was very helpful.

Without my knowledge, the late Judge Richard S. Arnold, then the Chief Judge of the Eighth Circuit Court of Appeals, wrote a letter to the Senate Judiciary Committee on my behalf. Almost a decade earlier, I had argued a case before the Eighth Circuit and Judge Arnold was one of the three judges on the panel. The very next day after the argument, I came across a case from the Third Circuit Court of Appeals that was diametrically opposed to my argument before the Eighth Circuit. I sent a letter to Judge Arnold and the other members of the panel with a copy of the Third Circuit's opinion that was contrary to my argument. Judge Arnold remembered that incident favorably and related it to the Senate Judiciary Committee in recommending that I be confirmed to the federal bench.

My confirmation hearing before the Senate Judiciary Committee was to be held in September 1993. Upon the date being set, Ms. Acheson scheduled meetings with her staff in Washington, D.C. to prep me for the hearing. My personal DAAG went over numerous questions, answers and scenarios with me. After two days, Ms. Acheson and four or five of her DAAGs sat me down and went round robin asking questions. I was well prepared for the confirmation hearing.

The day of the hearing arrived and my entourage included Kay, Kay's father's cousin Adelaide Henley (she and her husband Dr. Ben Henley had been our away-from-home parents in Washington, D.C.), and attorney Robert Sewell, who was my supervisor at the National Labor Relations Board and long-time pen pal. After we entered the hearing room, Missouri Senators John Danforth and Christopher "Kit" Bond and Congressman Bill Clay, Sr. soon appeared. They were followed by Illinois Senator Carol Moseley Braun who was to chair my judiciary subcommittee hearing. Senator Moseley Braun stated that the other two members of the subcommittee had been detained on other Senate business and would not be in attendance, so the hearing was slightly less intimidating than it might have been. I felt only a little nervous because I was so well prepared, and Kay and friends were there to support me. Once I learned that Senator Braun was subcommittee chair, I realized there was both Democratic and Republican support for my nomination and it was going to be smooth sailing. Senators Danforth and Bond, along with Congressman Clay, spoke of me in glowing terms. I made an opening statement and Senator Moseley Braun then asked me about ten questions. In half an hour it was over and all went well. I felt relieved.

With Senators Kit Bond and John Danforth, Kay and Bill Clay, Sr.

In mid-October, the Senate voted to confirm me for the position. On November 22, 1993, President William Jefferson Clinton signed my Commission as an Article III United States District Judge. It is the only document reflecting my qualifications that hangs in my chambers. The Presidential Commission says it all.

My Commission signed by President Bill Clinton

With Ronnie White, James Buford, Bill Clay, Sr. and Bernard
Shaw at the reception following my swearing-in ceremony

Soon after I was sworn in as a federal judge, I was scheduled to attend "baby judge school." This is where all newly commissioned federal judges are schooled on their responsibilities, federal law and procedure, sentencing guidelines, staffing and benefits. My group was made up of a number of bright, intelligent and politically well-connected individuals. Judge Billy Roy Wilson of Little Rock, who became known to me as "Wild Bill," was among the group. Kay and I subsequently visited Judge Wilson's Rasputin Mule Farm where I rode one of his mules.

Riding a Mule at the Rasputin Mule Farm

Judge Ginger Berrigan of New Orleans was another member of our group. Ginger and her husband Joe became great friends as our son

Bryan began attending college in New Orleans. Kay and I were their house guests on a number of occasions. They were wonderful hosts. Thanks so much.

Judge Ginger and Joe Berrigan

Judge Mark W. Bennett of Cedar Rapids, Iowa was also a member of our group. He has been an inspirational comrade with regard to the battle over federal sentencing guidelines.

Joining the Federal Bench

It was a blessing and bonus to become a federal judge. I always believed that the federal bench had a highly competent cadre of lawyers and a super support system. After I was appointed, my first task was to hire a staff. Carole Peek had been my secretary for most of my tenure as an Assistant U.S. Attorney, prior to her joining the staff of U.S. Magistrate Judge David Noce. She knew the system in and out. Carole agreed to be my judicial assistant. I knew I was in good hands.

Next I hired my first two law clerks. These are the judge's lawyers who do a great part of the legal lifting. They are essential for a judge to be right on the law. Susan Heider had worked with me on the state bench and I knew she did high quality work and was extremely competent. Attorney Levell Littleton calls her my "Super Duper." I agree. She is with me in chambers to this day. Craig Simmons was a young, bright and cheerful lawyer. He was working in New York and wanted to return to St. Louis. His school credentials were excellent and he came highly recommended. I felt he could do quality work and he did.

Carole, my judicial assistant, was an extension of me. She was a little older than me, wiser, and had real concern for me doing well. Before we started, Carole and I had a luncheon meeting with Susan and Craig. The four of us jelled quickly and were off and running. I was very comfortable with this staff, felt we could do quality work, and I believe we did.

With my Judicial Assistant Carole Peek, Al Erickson, Bernard Shaw and Law Clerk Craig Simmons

Current staff: (standing) Michele Crayton and Linda Errante Wehner
(seated) Law Clerks Lynn Reid, Susan Heider and Maggie Peters

My direction to staff was, and has always been, three things: First, we follow the law; second, make yourself happy; and third, don't let me do anything stupid. With these and other law clerks that joined my staff over the years, we have had extremely few reversals in civil cases. Criminal cases are another story. More on that later.

Welcome to the Big Time: The Smallest Courtroom Ever

When I moved across the street from the state Civil Courts Building into the old federal courthouse at Tucker and Market Streets in January 1994, it was like entering a more luxurious world. Although the federal courthouse was about the same age as the Civil Courts Building, both buildings having been completed in the early 1930s, the federal government obviously had more resources available for the upkeep and furnishing of its courthouse than the City of St. Louis did. The courtrooms were impressive and the judges' chambers were outstanding.

I don't know if my confirmation occurred more quickly than was expected, but the judge's chambers I was supposed to occupy was not ready, so my staff and I were temporarily placed in a small office on the fifth floor that belonged to an Eighth Circuit Court of Appeals senior judge whose home base was in Arkansas. I was assigned a tiny auxiliary courtroom in a back hall of the third floor, known as "Courtroom D." It was the smallest courtroom I had ever seen. When I stood up on the raised judge's bench area, my head almost brushed the ceiling. My friend, attorney Veo Peoples, told other associates of ours that although Charles was supposed to be this big-time federal judge, he was trying cases in a closet in the federal courthouse.

To get to Courtroom D, my staff and I would either walk down the back stairs or take the large freight elevator located in the back of the building by the loading dock. The elevator had a huge, openwork metal door that made a lot of noise as it came down and always landed with a solid jolt. Being in that elevator brought back vivid memories of my childhood some forty-five years before. When I was a small boy, perhaps five or six years old, Dad would sometimes bring me to his workplace at the Customs Office on the top floor of the building. More than anything else, I remember riding in that elevator, and thinking it was like a guillotine when the heavy door came down with a loud bang.

Shortly after I was sworn in, the other judges transferred 250 pending cases to me, many of them their cast-offs. I conducted hearings and held motion dockets in that tiny closet courtroom and sometimes it was overflowing with attorneys. I tried my first few federal cases in Courtroom D. One of the first cases was a patent case, tried without a jury in March 1994. This was my first federal non-jury trial. It was a hard-fought and well-litigated case about a pinless architectural hinge, and was actually one of my longer trials, lasting for sixteen days. If you've ever served on a jury, then you know it can be very hard to sit and listen to lawyers and witnesses all day for several days. Without a jury present, there was more pressure on me as the judge, and I was a little uncomfortable being the constant focus of numerous lawyers' attention and the sole audience for all of the evidence presented.

By the tenth day or so of trial, I wanted nothing more than to work hard and get the case completed as soon as possible, so I urged the lawyers to present as much of their evidence as they could each day. I also decided that in the future, I would have an advisory jury for all non-jury cases, which is a procedure that has worked well over the years.

I was ably assisted during the trial by my chief courtroom deputy clerk Michele Crayton, and I was grateful for her experience and professionalism. Michele and I knew each other from my time as an AUSA, but that had been some years prior and we hadn't had time to settle into a routine working relationship yet. One day as lunchtime approached, one of the lawyers approached Michele to inquire if they could take a break. Michele leaned over and very quietly asked if I was ready to break for lunch. I shook my head no, wanting to keep going.

A few minutes later, Michele noticed that a winged cockroach about three inches long was crawling along the floor. She didn't know where it was going and very much wanted to get away from it, but didn't want to ask me to stop because I had just said no to a break. If Michele had been a little more at ease with me at the time, she might have immediately gotten my attention, but under the circumstances she hesitated. So she said nothing, but put her hands on the thick court case file, thinking that if worse came to worse she could use it to swat the thing away if it came any closer. Sure enough, the cockroach suddenly appeared, crawling up the side of the clerk's area just next to where Michele was seated, which was on my right and below the bench area where I was seated.

Michele flicked the cockroach away with the edge of the file, sending it back to the floor. She glanced up at me on the bench to see if I had noticed her action, but I was watching the attorneys. As she looked up, she realized that several more large cockroaches were on the courtroom ceiling directly above me, like an insect Sword of Damocles. She reached up to the bench area and tapped gently, then pointed to the ceiling above my head. I looked up and immediately blurted out, "Oh my God, we're in recess!" I may well have cut an attorney off in mid-sentence in my hurry to get out of there and, if I did, I offer my apology now. I left Michele behind on my way out.

I wanted to have the trial moved to a different courtroom but that wasn't possible. I don't remember if it was later that day or the next day, but we were finally able to resume after building maintenance came and took care of the cockroach problem. My new building may have been nicer than the old Civil Court Building in many respects, but it would be hard to say which one had more cockroaches.

I had the good fortune to have Michele Crayton serve as my chief deputy clerk from 1994 to 2012. Michele is a consummate professional, and knows all there is to know about court and courtroom procedures. Michele provided me and my chambers staff with invaluable assistance and guidance, always given with poise and a smile. In 2012, Michele's superior skills were further recognized when she was promoted to the position of Deputy in Charge by the Clerk of Court. Jeff Jones has also been a long-term deputy clerk, serving with me from 1997 to the present. Jeff has always been a great asset to my office, as have a number of deputy clerks.

CHAPTER FIVE

Criminal Cases and the Sentencing Guidelines

Criminal cases and the constitutional issues they raise are, to me, the core of the judicial system. When a person is arrested and put on trial, and his or her liberty or even life is at stake, we engage in one of our most profoundly important activities as a society. For more than twenty-five years I presided over criminal cases and sentenced individuals in state and federal court. I felt a heavy burden of responsibility to impose a just and fair sentence, one that would serve to punish the crime and protect society but that was no harsher than necessary. Becoming a federal judge made this responsibility even more grave, given that my discretion to impose a just sentence was restricted by the mandatory federal sentencing guidelines.

When I left the U.S. Attorney's Office in 1987, the federal sentencing guidelines were just beginning to be implemented. Historically, judges had the ability to exercise their discretion to impose a sentence they thought was fair for the particular circumstances of the crime and the individual defendant. Congress adopted the guidelines with the intent to reduce the disparity between sentences that different criminal defendants received from different judges for committing the same crimes. Unfortunately, the guidelines did not have a beneficial result.

In November 2012, Senior U.S. Circuit Judge Myron H. Bright wrote in his dissenting opinion in *United States v. Spencer*, 700 F.3d 317 (8th Cir. 2012), "Since their adoption in 1987, many of the federal sentencing guidelines have proven unworkable, unfair, and have filled our federal prisons with defendants serving undeserved lengthy sentences, all at a higher cost to the government." Judge Bright stated that in 1984, almost half of federal defendants received a sentence of probation. By 2002, however, after the guidelines had been in effect for fifteen years, less than ten percent of federal defendants received a sentence of probation. Also, the average sentence imposed for all federal crimes almost doubled from 1984 to 1990, from twenty-four months to forty-six months. Just two years later, by 1992, the average sentence rose to almost sixty-seven months. The cost of incarcerating criminals in this country has increased steadily, and recent estimates put it at $75 billion per year. Over sixty percent of the prisoners in this country are nonviolent offenders.

I had no experience with the guidelines until 1994 when I took a seat on the federal bench and began to sentence federal defendants. In my years as a state court judge, I had sentenced hundreds of defendants using my best judgment and discretion. When I became a federal judge, the sentencing guidelines were considered mandatory, which meant that in almost all cases, I and other federal judges lacked the power to impose a sentence that fell outside the guidelines established under Congress's authority through the United States Sentencing Commission.

When I was assigned to a criminal division as a state court judge, many of the defendants who appeared before me were charged with violent crimes. It's not an exaggeration to say that a murder trial would begin in the circuit court of the City of St. Louis almost every week. Cases of murder, rape, aggravated assault, and unlawful use of a weapon were and are everyday occurrences there. Once I returned across the street and became a federal judge, the criminal cases were of a much different character. The bulk of the criminal cases in federal court in the Eastern District of Missouri involve guns and drugs: people charged with being a felon in possession of a firearm, or with possession of, or possession with the intent to distribute illegal drugs, primarily crack, methamphetamine or cocaine. Certainly there are many other types of criminal cases in federal court: identity theft, sex offenses including child pornography, white collar crimes such as embezzlement or securities fraud, wire fraud, robbery, kidnaping, arson, and some murder charges to name a few. The federal criminal code has expanded significantly in the last twenty years, so there are many more federal crimes now than there used to be. The bottom line, however, is that there is nowhere near the amount of violent crime charged in federal court as there is in the state court. Many of the defendants who appeared before me in federal court were nonviolent drug offenders, often addicts.

I was very unhappy with the mandatory sentencing guidelines because they removed my ability to use experience and discretion in fashioning a sentence that I felt fit the particular defendant and the crime. It seemed to me the guidelines often worked injustices in practice. As Judge Bright stated in *Spencer*, "In many cases, the guidelines do not present a reasonable starting point for sentencing decisions." Several federal appellate courts, however, including the Eighth Circuit Court of Appeals, had rejected challenges to the guidelines and determined that they were constitutional.

Court records show that as a federal judge I handled a total of 1,332 criminal cases involving over 1,785 defendants between 1994 and 2012. There were many times that I sentenced defendants within the mandatory sentencing guidelines range and felt I had imposed a fair sentence. I never hesitated to impose lengthy prison terms on violent individuals who had harmed others or were dangerous to society at large.

My disagreement with the guidelines usually arose in two situations: first, where I felt that the guidelines were too harsh when applied to the characteristics of the defendant before me and the particular circumstances of the crime committed. In some instances, my belief and judgment were that the defendant was a person for whom arrest had been a genuine wake-up call, a person who wanted to and was capable of change, of improving him or herself. Even though the defendant committed a serious crime, imposing a lengthy prison sentence was counterproductive and not the way to facilitate the needed change.

The second situation, which occurred much more frequently, was when I was required to sentence a nonviolent drug offender to a long mandatory guidelines sentence. This typically involved a young African-American male charged with a crack cocaine offense. The law provides very harsh sentences for crack cocaine offenses. For most of my tenure as a federal judge, the law required a defendant to possess 100 times as much powder cocaine to bring about the same penalty as for crack cocaine. The current ratio is eighteen to one. In general, African Americans tended to possess the cheaper crack cocaine, whereas white defendants more often possessed powder cocaine. As a result, I was required to sentence many nonviolent young black men to very long prison terms.

Most of these men came from single parent homes, with at least one parent or sibling in prison, and their presentence investigation reports almost uniformly recited a depressing litany of neglect or abuse suffered by them while growing up, sometimes almost unimaginable, as well as a lack of any support and positive guidance from adults in their lives. If you have children, think for a moment about how hard it was, how much care and how much time, effort and heartache it took to teach your children to behave, to learn, to achieve, to be responsible, and to do what is right. Think about how many times that child failed or did wrong, and you needed to provide continued and repeated guidance, punishment or encouragement, as appropriate. Then think about what a child might be like if he or she had been one of multiple children raised in poverty by a mentally ill or drug-addicted mother who didn't know or care if the child went to school, didn't provide regular meals or a safe, nurturing home environment, and emotionally neglected or perhaps even physically abused the child. Add into this picture growing up in a neighborhood where gang violence, rampant crime and drug use prevailed, and the child probably lived in fear of death or injury from violence either as an innocent bystander or a participant.

Many inner-city African-American young people have little hope for their future. They live in poverty without any of the trappings of the American dream. They drop out of school, or go through school with minimal effort, because they don't believe that academic exertion will make much difference in their lives. Most of the people who came before me in criminal cases had not completed high school. They had few, if any, skills that transfer to the job market. They become adolescent parents because they see no good reason for postponing or even being particularly careful with sexual activity. Uneducated and poorly educated people look to crime as the solution to their social and economic problems. They don't see any chance of obtaining success in the legitimate world. They sell drugs because the money they get allows them to obtain material possessions, power, recognition, and an escape from their world. Viewed through their eyes, the risks of arrest and jail seem small when measured against the rewards that selling drugs can bring them. These are the individuals taxpayers pay for twice, once for schools and social programs that fail, and a second time for incarcerating them.

This may surprise some people, but poor, African-American boys are often the most victimized because they are unwanted and often feared by society and employers. A young black male's chances of being murdered are many times greater than a white male's. Almost one-third of black men in their twenties in this country are either in jail or on probation or parole. Being imprisoned or without jobs, they are economically and socially useless to their families, to the mothers of their children, and as citizens in general. The boys often grow up fatherless, never learning what it means to be a responsible husband and father, so the cycle of uselessness, poverty and jail continues, generations leading lives without purpose.

These are the kinds of backgrounds I routinely saw in the people who came before me to be sentenced for drug crimes. What was the likelihood a person would have a chance to succeed in life with such a beginning? And many of them already had children of their own, whose futures were equally uncertain. In many of these cases, I believed that a long prison term would only teach these young men how to become better criminals and embitter and enrage them when, after enduring many years of dehumanizing conditions in confinement, they are returned to the streets as middle-aged men with little hope of obtaining legitimate employment. In the meantime, their families and community suffer from their absence, and taxpayers spend billions on building prisons and keeping more and more people incarcerated.

In December 1995, when I had been a federal judge for a little less than two years, I felt compelled to write a letter to the chairman of the U.S. Sentencing Commission, with a copy to President Clinton, to address the unfairness in the laws creating a disparity between sentences for powder and crack cocaine, and the disproportionate and negative effect the "war on drugs" was having on the black community, as well as its cost to society at large. (A copy of the letter is set out in the Appendix.) In April 2000, I wrote an editorial published in the *St. Louis Post-Dispatch* that decried the increasing incarceration of nonviolent offenders, primarily as a result of the war on drugs and mandatory minimum sentences and sentencing guidelines that punished crack cocaine offenses much more harshly than others. I pointed out that while crime rates were falling, the number of people incarcerated was rising, and that while African Americans accounted for fourteen percent of the nation's drug users, they made up thirty-five percent of those arrested for drug possession, fifty-five percent of those convicted for drug possession, and seventy-four percent of those sentenced to serve time. I noted the monetary cost of imprisoning nonviolent offenders, and pointed out that prison tends to turn inmates into "social misfits" who will likely return to crime. The number of federal prisoners increased from 21,539 in 1979 to 143,664 in 2004. Also from 1979 to 2004, the percentage of federal prisoners who are drug offenders increased from 25% to 55%. As of March 2013, the Federal Bureau of Prisons population has increased to 218,123, just under half of whom are incarcerated for drug offenses. As U.S. District Judge Mark W. Bennett astutely observed, "[T]he persistent ratcheting up of sentences for drug trafficking has done nothing to slow the tide of criminal activity. If harsh sentences actually worked this country—or at least the federal government—would have won the 'war on drugs' years ago. No one I know is even suggesting that we are holding our own in the war on drugs, let alone winning." *United States v. Beiermann*, 599 F. Supp. 2d 1087, 1103 (N.D. Iowa 2009).

When faced with having to impose a lengthy, mandatory sentence on a nonviolent offender, I often felt profound distress and frustration that my role as judge required me to take an action that I believed to be wrong and unjust. I often expressed disagreement with the mandatory sentencing guidelines to the AUSAs who prosecuted the cases. I complained in open court at sentencing hearings about my displeasure with the mandatory guidelines. I would say, "How could a 'guideline' be mandatory? We as lawyers are wordsmiths. 'Guideline' and 'mandatory' are conflicting terms. It doesn't make sense."

The AUSAs are the most respected government attorneys and prosecutors in the region. They have a difficult job but also have the best support and investigators in their arsenal. Every federal agency has special agents with investigative powers and specialized training, such as the FBI, Secret Service, IRS and DEA agents. They are the AUSAs' investigators. My seven years in the U.S. Attorney's Office was probably the most enjoyable and positive developmental period in my career. It was an honor to serve the United States, I respect that office and its attorneys. They are the good guys. But, Charles will be Charles, and as a judge I have had some conflicts with the office and some AUSAs over the years.

The AUSAs disliked my rants and pontificating about the guidelines. This was particularly so when I would complain that they were setting the mandatory sentence through their charging decisions. Many crimes can be charged in significantly different ways, and depending how the AUSA decides to charge the crime, the mandatory guidelines for sentencing are set and the judge has minimal discretion with respect to the ultimate sentence. (For readers who are interested in this issue, I recommend two books, *The Collapse of American Criminal Justice* by William J. Stuntz, and *The New Jim Crow: Mass Incarceration in the Age of Colorblindness* by Michelle Alexander.)

I would point out to the AUSAs that I as the judge, appointed by the President, confirmed by the U.S. Senate, having previously been a state court judge for more than six years and having had their position for seven years, was not making the sentencing decision. Instead, the prosecutors were really in charge of sentencing. I felt this picture was out of focus. The scales of justice were out of balance. I felt my role and experience qualified and obligated me to use my judgment to determine fair and adequate sentences, but the charging decisions and the sentencing guidelines took that authority away from me.

The AUSAs viewed my voicing of my opinion as demeaning and belittling of their authority. The AUSAs would sometimes respond that they could have charged a defendant with a harsher offense but chose not to, as a reason why I should sentence an individual at the top of the guideline sentencing range. I would respond with my friend and former St. Louis Cardinal Ted Savage's quip, "If a butterfly didn't have wings, they'd call him butty walker." In other words, the crime charged is what we have, not what could have been charged. I would add, "You didn't go for the harsher charge because you knew it was over the top." These episodes merely confirmed to me the AUSAs' control over sentencing.

The compulsory sentencing parameters stripped federal judges of any discretion and basically reduced us to postal mail sorters. When I worked for the post office while in college, I learned all the St. Louis city zip codes and the addresses in each. With this knowledge I sorted incoming mail and pigeonholed it into the appropriate slots. These were inside of boxes that looked like old wooden milk or soda crates with an individual slot for each zip code. Years later, it struck me that placing people's prison sentences within the narrow mandatory sentencing guidelines was comparable to placing mail in a predetermined slot. Instead of feeling like a federal judge, I felt as if I was back at the post office sorting mail.

The bottom line is that the AUSAs did not appreciate me robustly pointing out that they had more authority over sentencing than the judges. From time to time I would say to the AUSAs who had children that they knew from personal experience, people need to be treated as individuals. What is proper for one individual is often not appropriate for another, and successful outcomes demand varying, particularizing and individualizing one's approach. Their response to my observations and remarks was total silence.

Sometimes I would make another comparison. The "One Suit Fits All" story would be my analogy. What sense does it make for an individual to go into a clothing store and be told that there is only one size suit in the store and that's what they have to wear? People are distinct individuals with different characteristics, backgrounds, and crime scenarios. But under the mandatory guidelines defendants had to wear the same size suit whether it fit or not. The AUSAs, trial judges and appellate judges were tailors of but one sized suit for all. And I was part of the scheme, too. Even though I was vocal in my objections, I was still working at the tailor shop.

Despite having been an attorney for twenty years with significant prosecutorial and judicial experience sentencing hundreds if not thousands of people in state court, I had almost no discretion in federal sentencing. In my experience, the AUSAs would vehemently object if I chose to sentence a defendant below the guidelines, and would appeal my sentence to the U.S. Court of Appeals for the Eighth Circuit. In most instances, the Court of Appeals would reverse any below-guidelines sentence and remand it with directions to impose a guideline sentence. At the same time, they would often affirm sentences above the guidelines range.

In *United States v. Meyers*, 452 F.3d 998 (8th Cir. 2006), the late Senior U.S. Circuit Judge Gerald W. Heaney, writing for himself, observed that in the year and a half since the sentencing guidelines had been declared advisory, the Eighth Circuit affirmed twelve sentences that exceeded the recommended guidelines range, but reversed only one. In contrast, when sentences were imposed below the recommended guidelines range during that same period, the Eighth Circuit reversed sixteen of the sentences and affirmed only three. Judge Heaney concluded, "Affirming upward variances at a rate of 92.3% while affirming downward variances at a rate of 15.8% could hardly be viewed as uniform treatment, and seems contrary to 18 U.S.C. § 3553(a)(6)'s concern with eliminating unwarranted sentencing disparity . . . . It is difficult to accept that § 3553(a)(6) is satisfied where a circuit treats sentencing appeals in a consistently disparate manner."

In 2005, the Supreme Court held in *United States v. Booker*, 543 U.S. 200, that the guidelines were advisory and could not be treated as mandatory. Even after the guidelines were deemed advisory, during sentencing proceedings, the AUSAs uniformly recommended sentencing a defendant within the guideline range. In 2007, the Supreme Court held in *Rita v. United States*, 551 U.S. 338, that federal trial courts cannot "presume that a sentence within the applicable guidelines range is reasonable." Even after the guidelines were held not to be presumptively reasonable, the AUSAs continued to ask that I impose the guideline range for the defendants who came before me. It was remarkable how the AUSAs consistently came to the conclusion that the advisory sentencing guidelines range was the only reasonable sentencing range. According to them, the present case was always the case where the circumstances required the guideline range. I would occasionally tell the AUSA on such a case, "Since you always recommend a guideline sentence we don't even need your presence. We could just play your tape. When you have a recommendation outside the guidelines, show up and tell me what it is." It was the same old song every time. They never were able to point to a case where they recommended below the guidelines.

The Supreme Court made it clear long ago that federal prosecutors are held to a higher standard of care than other attorneys, as they are charged to do justice: "The United States Attorney is the representative not of an ordinary party to a controversy, but of a sovereignty whose obligation to govern impartially is as compelling as its obligation to govern at all; and whose interest, therefore, in a criminal prosecution is not that it shall win a case, but that justice shall be done." *Berger v. United States*, 295 U.S. 78, 88 (1935). Similarly, the Eighth Circuit has stated, "The prosecutor's special duty as a government agent is not to convict, but to secure justice." *United States v. O'Connell*, 841 F.2d 1408 (8th Cir. 1988). The United States Department of Justice's mission statement includes these principles: "to seek just punishment for those guilty of unlawful behavior; and to ensure fair and impartial administration of justice for all Americans."

U.S. District Judge Mark W. Bennett wrote this about the U.S. Attorney's Office in the Northern District of Iowa where he sits: "I posit then, that if this United States Attorney's Office took its mission to do justice in sentencings as seriously as it takes its desire to obtain convictions, its application of the [statutory sentencing] factors to every defendant with a guideline range above a mandatory minimum could not result in so few cases in which a downward variance was deemed acceptable." *United States v. Beiermann*, 599 F. Supp. 2d 1087 (N.D. Iowa 2009). I concur fully with Judge Bennett's statement. I was disappointed that despite the changes in the sentencing guidelines, the AUSAs generally never had a recommendation for sentencing below the advisory guidelines. The U.S. Justice Department is charged with doing justice. Advocating that every defendant should be sentenced within the guidelines does not constitute justice.

In 2005, after the guidelines were determined to be advisory, one of the brightest AUSAs in the courthouse was in my courtroom for a guilty plea proceeding. The defendant had been charged with six small drug sales to undercover DEA agents. This was unusual, as there are generally only one, two, or occasionally three buys before the perpetrator is arrested. I expressed concern that the DEA agents intentionally allowed the number of sales to increase prior to arresting the defendant in order to subject him to a longer mandatory sentence. The AUSA was so upset by my statements that she couldn't cogently respond or explain why prosecutorial action had not been taken sooner as to this low-level drug dealer. I then suggested that perhaps the DEA agents should be charged with conspiracy for keeping a drug dealer on our streets. It was likely the first time that this very bright, articulate, well-prepared AUSA had been publicly confronted with the unfairness of a prosecution. I hope my comments caused her to think about the gravitas of the charging decisions she makes.

Sometimes I would complain to the AUSAs that they were seeking harsh mandatory sentences for young men who would still be young when their time had been served. I expressed concern that a number of them would grow bitter and become better criminals in prison, and when released they would return to a community not where the AUSA lived, but where people like my parents lived, who might be victims of these hardened individuals' wrath. I don't believe this hit home with any of the AUSAs. This was not something that had meaning to them in their lives.

When the Supreme Court finally decided in 2005 that the federal sentencing guidelines were merely advisory rather than mandatory, nearly twenty years after they were established, some degree of sanity and balance was restored. Before that decision, one of my fellow judges said to me, "Charles, your problem is that you don't believe in the guidelines." That's true, and I had expressed those sentiments to the U.S. Sentencing Commission and President Clinton shortly after I became a federal judge, ten years before the Supreme Court's long-overdue decision. After the guidelines were declared advisory, I never heard from the judge who said my problem was not believing in the guidelines.

It is a very good thing that the guidelines were finally declared advisory, but by that time a large number of federal judges sitting on the bench had no sentencing experience apart from the mandatory guidelines and, therefore, no other sentencing frame of reference. This is a serious concern because these judges lack experience in using their discretion to impose an appropriate and fair sentence on a defendant, based on that defendant's characteristics and the facts of the individual case. Such judges are much more likely to impose a sentence within the now-advisory guidelines because this is all they know. I have raised this concern with colleagues, but have gotten little response.

Even though many of the people who came before me on drug charges were nonviolent offenders, and often were simply drug users and addicts, the sentences I was required to impose on these people were as long as or longer than sentences I had imposed for violent criminals that I felt presented a real danger to society. It weighs heavily on my conscience that I have been a part of a judicial system that has put low-level drug users and sellers in prison for many years, sometimes for decades. I would very much like to see the Eastern District of Missouri develop a drug court pretrial diversion program, as some other federal courts are now doing, that would treat low-level drug users and sellers as needing treatment rather than imprisonment.

In such a program, the AUSAs would forego charging the offenders and they would be closely supervised, provided treatment to cure their addictions, and given support and encouragement to enable them to obtain education and employment. This would give offenders the tools to earn a legitimate living, and offer a real alternative to selling and using drugs as an occupation and lifestyle. Drug diversion programs are at the forefront of change in the judicial system, and I believe they will reduce substance abuse, crime and recidivism, and save vast amounts of taxpayer money. Supervision is much less expensive than incarceration, and it can prevent the horrendous human costs of broken families and wasted lives that are associated with the long-term incarceration of drug addicts and low-level offenders.

Don't get me wrong, I do believe incarceration is needed for drug offenders in many instances, especially where dealers use guns and violence in committing their crimes. Even in the majority of those cases, however, I believe the offender will have paid his or her debt to society, become sober, and be ready to rejoin society in five to seven years. As of 2010, almost half of federal drug offenders were convicted of an offense with a ten-year mandatory minimum sentence. Over forty percent were subject to a five-year minimum. Just over five percent were subject to mandatory minimum sentences of twenty years or life in prison. Sentences of thirty years to life are not unusual for repeat offenders sentenced as career offenders. These overly long sentences for drug crimes represent a "tough on crime" political viewpoint that has not worked to solve the drug problem in our country over the past thirty years. Federal sentences for drug offenders are harsh and unjust, and simply bad for our society and economy. I believe that we as a society are just now beginning to change our overall attitudes about lengthy sentences for drug offenders and other punitive laws such as three-strikes provisions, and I strongly believe this is a step in the right direction.

When I took senior status in 2010 I made the choice not to take any more criminal cases. The criminal cases weighed heavily on me, and even after the more recent Supreme Court decisions returning some sentencing discretion to the trial judge, I still felt like a cog in the machine, as almost every below-guidelines sentence I imposed was appealed to the Eighth Circuit and even the Supreme Court. I was tired of defending my below-guidelines sentences, while judges who continue to sentence at or above the guidelines were given a pass. I have sent too many people to prison for too long, and my conscience will not allow me to do it any longer. So I no longer sentence criminal defendants, and I'm glad to have retired from making so many suits that didn't fit. The AUSAs are happy and so am I. It is all good.

* * *

On August 12, 2013, while I was finishing this book, U.S. Attorney General Eric Holder issued a Memorandum to the United States Attorneys, which belatedly established a national charging policy on mandatory minimum sentences for certain nonviolent, low-level drug offenders and on recidivist enhancements. The Memorandum says in part, "We must ensure that our most severe mandatory minimum penalties are reserved for serious, high-level, or violent drug traffickers." I welcome and am greatly encouraged by this change in national policy. These goals can only be reached, however, if the new policy is implemented in all ninety-four U.S. Attorneys' offices across the country, and followed by each and every AUSA.

*   *   *

When I was faced with sentencing a defendant under the mandatory sentencing guidelines and felt the sentence was unjust for that particular defendant's crime and situation, I would make every effort to find a way to lower the sentence, but this was often impossible. Sometimes, all I could do was speak to the defendant on a level that he or she could understand, not using lawyer words and an attitude of superiority or condescension, but rather using language of the street, as a person who could relate to the circumstances of their lives.

Judge Clyde Cahill, God rest his gentle soul, personalized his sentences. As a federal judge, he talked to defendants as people, trying to redirect these wayward individuals. This approach engendered detractors in the courthouse, particularly among the AUSAs. But he was trying to save souls. Hopefully he did, but only God knows for sure. I, too, talked to some defendants at sentencing hoping to save and redirect wayward souls.

As judges, we are sentencing real individuals, not statistics, and I think if you can give defendants advice for changing their lives, all the better. When I was a federal prosecutor, I did not think highly of a sentencing when the judge did not talk to the person to be sentenced. Often it seemed as though the judge was merely making a record for the appellate court, unconcerned about the future of the defendant.

As a judge, I chose to talk to some defendants, particularly African-American young men who might identify with me, might be redirected, and might be amenable to my advice.

Here is some of the advice I frequently gave defendants:

- You have to make good use of the time you are serving. Improve your body and mind. Exercise, get in better physical shape. Get an education. Work on getting your GED. Learn a trade. You need to be a better person after serving your time.

- When you can read and write, we all know each other. (This was a saying of my friend, the late Dr. Clyde Stockton of Columbia, South Carolina.)

- When you go to the penitentiary you will meet people with all kinds of schemes. Don't get yourself in more trouble following them. Ask yourself, "If they are so slick, what are they doing here?"

- If you continue to commit these small crimes, you will be doing a life sentence on the installment plan. (This is an aphorism I borrowed from the late Judge Kenneth Wangelin and that fellow U.S. District Judge Rodney W. Sippel also employs.)

- You are the only person in this courtroom dressed in a funny outfit. All of us, me, the prosecutor, your attorney, the probation officer, the marshals, the court reporter, the courtroom clerk, are getting paid (cha-ching) because of you. You need to fire us.

- You must change your ways in order to be a better father, be an advisor to your children and be a useful citizen. You will find it extremely difficult if not impossible to do any of these things if you are incarcerated.

- Only you can make the change in your life. You have to help yourself. Nobody can do it but you, the man in the mirror.

There were times when it was possible to impose a below-guidelines sentence, but such sentences were often appealed by the government and, more often than not, reversed by the Eighth Circuit Court of Appeals. In each of those cases, I believed that the sentence I imposed was the right sentence for the particular defendant and the circumstances of the case. Despite the fact that I was reversed fairly often in criminal cases, I continued to sentence people as individuals to the best of my ability, as that was the right thing to do. The following are some of the criminal cases that were particularly significant to me and illustrate my efforts to follow both the law and my conscience in carrying out my duties.

United States v. Feemster
Career Offenders and Crack Cocaine

A case involving a defendant named Kendrix Feemster exemplifies my attempts to sentence fairly under the advisory guidelines scheme. The case's procedural history spanned several years in which the new jurisprudence of the advisory guidelines was being developed by the federal courts. Mr. Feemster was convicted in 2005, at the age of twenty-six, of distributing a total of eighteen grams of crack cocaine on two occasions. (A gram of cocaine is about the equivalent in size to a packet of artificial sweetener, or about a quarter of a teaspoon. A gram of crack cocaine would be of similar size but in a hard nugget or "rock" form. As a reference, a Life Savers candy weighs about two grams.)

Under the advisory guidelines, Mr. Feemster's range of punishment was 92 to 115 months of imprisonment, a period of approximately seven and a half to nine and a half years. This seemed about right to me. However, Mr. Feemster had a lengthy criminal history mostly made up of petty crime convictions. Unfortunately for him, two of his crimes qualified as felony crimes of violence, which made him a "career offender" under the guidelines. One of the crimes of violence was a first-degree burglary committed when he was seventeen, but for which he was prosecuted as an adult and served four and a half years of a six-year sentence. The other qualifying offense was a first-degree robbery committed at the age of twenty-three for which he was sentenced to ten years, but execution of the sentence was suspended and he was placed on probation. As a result of these two prior convictions, Mr. Feemster's sentencing range more than tripled, increasing to 360 months (thirty years) to life in prison based, in part, on acts committed while a juvenile.

He was also subject to a ten-year mandatory minimum sentence because of a felony drug crime committed when he was sixteen, but for which he was prosecuted as an adult.

Under the applicable federal statute, a sentencing judge in determining the correct sentence must consider the following factors: the nature and circumstances of the offense and the history and characteristics of the defendant, the need for the sentence imposed to reflect the seriousness of the offense, to promote respect for the law, and to provide just punishment, to provide adequate deterrence, to protect the public, to provide the defendant with educational or vocational training, medical care, or other corrective treatment in the most effective manner, the kinds of sentences available, the sentencing guideline range and any policy statements, the need to avoid unwarranted sentencing disparities, and the need to provide restitution to the victims.

With these factors in mind, prior to the sentencing I carefully reviewed the Presentence Investigation Report (PSR) prepared by the Federal Probation Office that discussed Mr. Feemster's background in detail, so I was completely familiar with his prior criminal record as well as his personal background, including his family, medical and educational history. In addition, of course, I had heard the evidence presented at trial. My conclusion was that although Mr. Feemster had engaged in significant criminal behavior and was definitely on the wrong path in life, much of his criminal activity had occurred while he was a teen. I also considered the fact that he had a history of drug and alcohol abuse dating back to the age of twelve, and that he had not used a weapon in his crimes.

It was troubling that the harsh thirty years to life guidelines sentence was triggered in part by a crime committed when Mr. Feemster was only seventeen, and that he would be at least fifty-four years old when he was eventually released. This was a situation where a young man who was primarily a petty criminal was going to be locked up for thirty-plus years at taxpayer expense. Mr. Feemster struck me as a person whose life had some potential and it seemed too early to give up on him, to write off at least thirty years of his life, if not his entire life, at age twenty-six, based on the final straw of selling eighteen grams of crack cocaine.

I concluded that imposing a concurrent ten-year (120 month) mandatory minimum sentence on each of the two counts and eight years of supervised release would deter Mr. Feemster from criminal conduct and would send a message to the community that the courts will punish those who sell illegal drugs on the streets. Incarceration would also offer him the ability to obtain drug and alcohol abuse treatment, and obtain educational and vocational training to supplement his tenth-grade education and GED, perhaps giving him a better chance to lead a law-abiding life after his release.

The government appealed the sentence and the Eighth Circuit Court of Appeals remanded the case to me, saying that for it to affirm such a large variance from the advisory guidelines range, i.e., 120 months instead of 360, I had to provide a "more explicit and thorough consideration" of all the relevant sentencing factors that went into my decision. After the remand, I conducted another sentencing hearing and explained my decision more fully, noted the additional consideration that Mr. Feemster had successfully completed two terms of probation, and then reimposed the 120-month term of imprisonment and eight years of supervised release. The government appealed again, this time asking that the judgment be reversed and including the uncommon request that the case be remanded to a different judge. On this appeal, the Eighth Circuit reversed, stating that in sentencing Mr. Feemster I gave too much weight to his age at the time of the offense and at the time of his prior offenses, that it was improper to consider the facts that he had not used weapons and had successfully completed two terms of probation, and that I had not given sufficient weight to the need to avoid unwarranted sentencing disparities.

Mr. Feemster appealed the reversal of his sentence to the U.S. Supreme Court, which vacated the Eighth Circuit's decision and remanded the case back to that court for further consideration in light of *Gall v. United States*, 552 U.S. 38 (2007). The *Gall* decision held that when an appeals court reviews the reasonableness of a sentence that is outside the guidelines range, it may take the degree of variance into account, but there is no rule that requires a district court to find "extraordinary circumstances" to justify a sentence outside the guidelines range.

On remand from the Supreme Court, the Eighth Circuit again reversed my decision, holding that the 120-month sentence was an abuse of discretion. The Eighth Circuit said that while it was proper to consider Mr. Feemster's status as a juvenile at the time of some prior convictions, it was improper to consider his age at the time of the offense, the fact that he had not carried a weapon, and his successful completion of two terms of probation. Mr. Feemster moved for a rehearing by the Eighth Circuit en banc, meaning that all the judges of the Court would consider the case, and the rehearing was granted, something that happens only a few times each year in the Eighth Circuit.

Finally, the en banc Eighth Circuit affirmed the sentence, concluding I had adequately explained my decision to impose concurrent 120-month sentences on Mr. Feemster, and that the sentence itself was not substantively unreasonable. I was relieved the case would not come back to me and that Mr. Feemster would not receive an over the top sentence. Mr. Feemster was released from prison in July 2013. I fervently hope he will be able to begin a life free of criminal conduct, with the help and support of our district's fine Probation Office. I will always believe it would have been wrong, unjust and immoral to incarcerate him for thirty years to life as he first stood before me for sentencing. Nevertheless, Mr. Feemster's future is in his own hands.

United States v. Collier
Crack Amendment Resentencing

In November 2007, the U.S. Sentencing Commission amended the sentencing guidelines to lower the disparity between sentences for powder cocaine and crack cocaine. This reduced the base offense level for crack cocaine by two sentencing levels, and was applied retroactively. As a result, many defendants convicted of offenses involving crack cocaine were entitled to seek to have their prison sentences reduced. Even with this amendment, defendants convicted of crack cocaine offenses still had to serve longer sentences than those convicted of powder cocaine offenses, but it was a valuable step in the right direction. Many of the defendants I had sentenced on crack cocaine charges had already served their full sentences, but for those I could help by imposing a more just sentence, I did. Without exception, I reduced the prison sentence of every defendant who sought the reduction and met the qualifications.

The sentencing commission identified one group of individuals that did not meet the qualifications. If a defendant was sentenced for an offense involving crack cocaine, and was found to be a career offender under the sentencing guidelines based on his criminal history, he would not be entitled to a sentence reduction under the new guidelines for crack cocaine offenses. Often times in sentencings I had found that the career offender status over-represented a particular defendant's criminal history. For example, if a criminal defendant had a strong work history, education, or record of military service, suffered from mental disorders or drug addiction, or was relatively young at the time of prior drug-related offenses, I might conclude that the career offender status was not warranted. In these instances, I would sentence the criminal defendant based on the drug quantity table, and not on his status as a career offender, which would result in a shorter sentence.

One defendant I remember in particular was Robert Collier, who was an atypical drug offender. After graduating from high school, he served in the United States Army and Army Reserves for ten years and was honorably discharged. Mr. Collier had worked and supported his family. He also suffered depression and post-traumatic stress disorder, and admitted self-medicating with alcohol and cocaine. Mr. Collier's first arrest, on an attempted burglary charge, occurred when he was thirty-four. In the next few years, he was convicted three times on drug-related charges, including the possession and sale of crack cocaine. While in state prison, he participated in substance abuse treatment and after his release completed outpatient drug treatment, attended Narcotics Anonymous and was in counseling to deal with his depression, but could not stay clean.

Because Mr. Collier had prior drug convictions, he was considered a career offender under the guidelines when he came before me in 2005 to be sentenced for possession with the intent to distribute crack cocaine. If he had not been classified as a career offender, he would have been subject to a minimum term of 60 months imprisonment, but as a career offender the guidelines range was 188 to 235 months, or fifteen to almost twenty years. Based on Mr. Collier's history and circumstances, I determined that the career offender designation substantially over-represented his criminal history, and that he should be sentenced to 72 months imprisonment and participate in an intensive drug treatment program while incarcerated. The government appealed and the Eighth Circuit reversed, finding this sentence was substantively unreasonable. Following remand I sentenced Mr. Collier to 120 months.

In 2008, Mr. Collier moved to have his sentence reduced under the amended guidelines for crack cocaine offenses. Although the amended guidelines did not apply to career offenders, I did not believe I had sentenced Mr. Collier under the career offender guideline, but instead had determined that the career offender designation was inappropriate because it substantially over-represented his criminal history. I concluded Mr. Collier's sentence had been based instead on the drug quantity table, and that it was within my discretion whether to grant him a sentence reduction. I exercised that discretion and reduced his sentence to 70 months.

The government appealed this reduced sentence, arguing simply that the amendments to the sentencing guidelines for crack cocaine offenses did not apply to career offenders, and that Mr. Collier had been sentenced as a career offender despite the fact that I sentenced him below the guidelines range. The Eighth Circuit agreed and reversed Mr. Collier's 70-month reduced sentence. I was required to reinstate his 120-month sentence.

This case was a disappointment. Twice I felt I had the discretion to sentence Mr. Collier to a term of imprisonment less than 120 months, first at his sentencing and then after the amendments were passed to lower the disparity between crack and powder cocaine offenses. I exercised every bit of discretion I had for Mr. Collier, a nonviolent drug offender whose main problems seemed to be his addiction and depression, but to no avail. The unfortunate irony is that his time honorably serving this country in the Army will be matched by his time spent in prison.

United States v. Kane
Post-Sentencing Rehabilitation

Another case that was strongly affected by the changing status of the sentencing guidelines involved Ruth Kane, a sorry soul who traded the sexual abuse of her young daughter for alcohol, money and food. In 2003, Ms. Kane was charged with one count of conspiracy to commit aggravated abuse with a child under the age of twelve, and six counts of aggravated sexual abuse of a child under the age of twelve.

Ms. Kane was a drug addict and alcoholic with some indication of mental illness. She was played upon, used, by her co-defendant, a pedophile named Joseph Champion who took advantage of her addiction and weakness to get at her daughter. This pedophile was called "Santa Claus" by the neighborhood children because he always came with gifts, candy and rode them around on his Harley. Ms. Kane allowed and assisted this pedophile in having repeated sexual contact with her daughter for a two-year period when the girl was nine to ten years old. Ms. Kane's conduct was extremely serious, unquestionably vile and reprehensible, and a violation of every kind of parental duty and instinct. Nonetheless, I believed that the pedophile's actions were more serious, and more vile and reprehensible, because he carefully planned his crimes, took advantage of and played upon Ms. Kane's weaknesses, and subjected her to his control.

The pedophile pleaded guilty and I sentenced him to 180 months imprisonment, which was within the mandatory sentencing range of 168 to 210 months. He would have faced a sentencing range of 292 to 365 months if he had not pleaded guilty, as the guidelines significantly increase the penalties for those who exercise their right to trial. Ms. Kane chose to go to trial, and the jury found her guilty on only two of the seven counts of the indictment. I sentenced her to 210 months imprisonment, which was at the bottom of the mandatory sentencing range of 210 to 262 months. It bothered me greatly that I had to sentence Ms. Kane to a longer prison term than the pedophile, as I felt that his conduct was significantly worse than hers, and she had been under his control. Ms. Kane was subject to a longer sentence under the guidelines than the pedophile for the <u>sole</u> reason that she chose to exercise her constitutional right to a jury trial.

While Ms. Kane's sentence was on appeal in 2005, the U.S. Supreme Court declared in *Booker* that the sentencing guidelines were advisory. As a result, the Eighth Circuit sent Ms. Kane's case back to me, because I had said during her sentencing that if the guidelines were not mandatory, I might do something different. When the case returned to me for resentencing and I saw Ruth Kane again, I was struck by how markedly different she appeared. Her demeanor, alertness and appearance were greatly improved since the time of her sentencing, and it was obvious to me that something positive had been happening in her life while she was in prison. I learned that Ms. Kane had obtained her GED and took 80 hours of parenting classes and almost 600 hours of vocational training while in prison which was a significant effort at self-improvement. I decided that she should be given consideration for post-sentencing rehabilitation and sentenced her to 120 months, 60 months less than the 180 months of her co-defendant, the manipulating pedophile. It was still a long sentence, ten years, and longer than what she would have received in state court.

The U.S. Attorney's Office objected to this sentence, appealed, and the Eighth Circuit reversed, stating that the 90-month reduction in sentencing was too lenient and that no consideration could be given for post-sentencing rehabilitation. Ms. Kane appealed to the Supreme Court, which vacated the reversal and directed the Eighth Circuit to reconsider. The Eighth Circuit reconsidered and again reversed the 120-month sentence. Ms. Kane again appealed to the Supreme Court, which again vacated the Eighth Circuit's decision and directed it to consider the Supreme Court's recent decision in *Pepper v. United States*, that post-sentencing rehabilitation was indeed an appropriate factor a judge could take into consideration when fashioning a sentence.

Following the Supreme Court's second decision, the Eighth Circuit reexamined the reasonableness of the 120-month sentence. The Eighth Circuit's opinion described at great length the horrendous nature of Ms. Kane's offense and the number of times the abuse of her daughter occurred, and therefore concluded my sentence was unreasonable. The opinion gave short shrift to Ms. Kane's rehabilitation and what she had done in prison. The opinion also did not mention that by the time it was issued, Ms. Kane had served her sentence, was released from prison, had obtained a job, and had begun rebuilding a relationship with her daughter. It was obvious that the factors I found important in sentencing Ruth Kane meant nothing to the appellate judges who had never seen her.

Being a trial judge, listening to numerous witnesses, criminal defendants and lawyers, you get a real sense for people and their character. Acting as the referee, I was on the field in the midst of the action watching, listening, comparing and ruling as to witnesses and evidence. Appellate judges, on the other hand, sit in the skybox luxury seats and thereafter, in effect, make credibility rulings. It has been said that you can tell if some people are lying because their lips are moving. When you're sitting in the upper deck skybox, why even try it? You are too far removed from the action to determine credibility. As singer James Brown was pointing out when he declared, "Give the drummer some," give some deference, respect, credit and significant consideration to the person carrying the basic beat, the trial judge.

On the final remand of Ms. Kane's case to me, the government would not agree to a sentence of time served, but did ultimately agree that Ruth Kane should serve a sentence of 146 months. Unfortunately, Ms. Kane was required to return to prison to serve the additional time, disrupting her life as a sober, productive member of society. She is scheduled for release in early 2015. What a waste of time, money, and resources the multiple *Kane* appeals were. I am thankful, though that Ms. Kane, who has made such positive strides in her life, and I hope will continue to do so, was not required to serve the entirety of the original 210-month sentence.

United States v. Lazaroff
Fraud and a Criticized Sentence

Another criminal case, this one occurring while the sentencing guidelines were mandatory, was memorable because of the publicity associated with it. Michael K. Lazaroff was a prominent wheeler-dealer lawyer who was a partner at a large downtown St. Louis law firm. He came from a privileged background and was known for representing casino interests and raising funds for Democratic political candidates. Mr. Lazaroff took a large amount of legal fees from a client and hid them from his law firm, solicited illegal campaign contributions from fellow lawyers and staff, and was caught and paid the price. In 2000, Mr. Lazaroff was charged with two counts of fraud and one count of making false material statements, and pleaded guilty under a plea agreement. The mandatory guidelines sentencing range was 27 to 33 months.

Attorney Art Margulis represented Mr. Lazaroff and an experienced AUSA represented the government. They met with me in chambers prior to the sentencing. The AUSA had filed what is known as a 5K1 motion under the sentencing guidelines. A 5K1 motion is filed at the government's discretion in cases where the defendant has cooperated with the government by providing substantial assistance in the investigation or prosecution of other cases. Mr. Lazaroff cooperated by providing information concerning alleged violations of Missouri law by individuals and corporations involved in the casino gaming industry. The government's filing of this motion gave me the rare opportunity to depart from the mandatory guidelines and impose the sentence I thought was appropriate. The AUSA urged me to sentence Mr. Lazaroff to one year in jail and attorney Margulis pushed for probation.

The government and Margulis provided a number of letters from public officials, friends, and pillars of the community concerning Mr. Lazaroff, a common practice prior to sentencings. Among the letters the government provided was one from the FBI case agent. The agent praised Mr. Lazaroff and his cooperation efforts in glowing terms, indicating Mr. Lazaroff had done everything that was asked of him and more. In my years on the bench, I had never before received such a favorable letter from an FBI case agent regarding a defendant's level of cooperation in an investigation. I was persuaded, primarily by this letter but also by others submitted on Mr. Lazaroff's behalf, that the sentence I intended to impose was just and appropriate.

The AUSA acknowledged that by filing the 5K1 motion, the government gave me complete discretion to craft whatever sentence I found appropriate, but he still wanted Mr. Lazaroff to serve that one year in jail. The AUSA stated in chambers, though, that whatever I did would be acceptable, and nothing would be said about it. We went out to the courtroom and his exact words on the record were, "Whatever your sentence is the government will accept it and respect it. You will not hear the government criticize your sentence in the press or anywhere else for that matter." I sentenced Mr. Lazaroff to thirty days in jail on work release, ninety days of home confinement, three years of supervised release, 120 hours of community service, and payment of restitution to his law firm in the amount of $765,740.40. Mr. Lazaroff also lost his license to practice law. The government did not think this was enough.

After I handed down the sentence, the AUSA did criticize it, complaining to the press that he had "requested real jail time" and "a halfway house was not what we had in mind by real jail." The *St. Louis Post-Dispatch* ate it up with gusto, stating in a lead editorial on October 5, 2000 that the sentence was a miscarriage of justice imposed by a "Democratic judge," a blatant accusation of cronyism. The *Post* also mentioned my writing of editorials criticizing the long sentences given to young African-American men in drug cases, and attempted to portray me as a hypocrite by pointing out that on the same day I sentenced Mr. Lazaroff, I gave a nine-month sentence to a black female crack addict. The next day the *Post* acknowledged its mistake, the crack addict was actually a white woman. The *Post* also failed to mention or recognize the key distinction between the cases: I had no discretion to sentence the crack addict defendant to anything less than the mandatory sentence called for by the guidelines, as was so often the case.

Whitfield v. Bowersox
The Constitutional Right to Testify

One of the most rewarding cases I handled on the federal bench was a petition for writ of habeas corpus filed by a Missouri death-row inmate named Joseph Whitfield. Federal habeas cases are civil cases, but they are based on underlying criminal cases. If a person is convicted of a crime in state court and has exhausted all of the appeals allowed under state law, he can challenge the conviction or sentence in federal court on the basis that it violated some aspect of his constitutional rights. Many of these habeas cases are filed, both by state and federal prisoners, but relief is seldom granted.

Mr. Whitfield was convicted of first-degree murder, assault and armed criminal action in the circuit court of the City of St. Louis in 1994. There are two phases to a first-degree murder prosecution in Missouri where the state is seeking the death penalty. In the first phase of the trial, the jury determines guilt. In the second phase, additional evidence is presented and the jury determines the penalty or punishment to be assessed, which is limited to either life in prison without parole or death. The jury convicted Mr. Whitfield of first-degree murder and armed criminal action, but could not agree on punishment during the penalty phase and voted eleven to one in favor of life imprisonment. Because the jury could not agree, a Missouri statute required the trial judge to undertake a four-step process to determine punishment. The judge did so, and sentenced Mr. Whitfield to death. Mr. Whitfield's appeal and motion for post-conviction relief were denied. The Missouri Supreme Court affirmed, meaning that Mr. Whitfield's execution could be scheduled.

In 1997, Mr. Whitfield filed a federal habeas petition and it was assigned to me. Like most habeas cases, the case raised numerous grounds and claims for setting aside the conviction and sentence. Death penalty habeas cases in particular are known for taking a great deal of time and effort to resolve because of the number of claims they usually contain, the importance of the issues as a person's life is literally at stake, and because the cases have a long procedural history in multiple levels of state court with records and transcripts that must be carefully reviewed and examined.

In August 2000, I decided in a lengthy written opinion that Mr. Whitfield's habeas petition should be denied in all respects. Mr. Whitfield's attorneys filed a motion that urged me to reconsider my denial with respect to three of his claims. After very careful consideration, I decided in January 2001 that I had been wrong to deny one of Mr. Whitfield's claims. I concluded that Mr. Whitfield's fundamental constitutional right to testify during the penalty phase of his trial was violated because he asked to testify twice but was not allowed to. I also concluded that his trial attorney was constitutionally ineffective because she failed to defend and ensure his right to testify at the penalty phase.

The right to testify is one of the most well-established and fundamental constitutional rights. Because the right is so fundamental, only the defendant can waive it, not his attorney and not the judge. It was clear that Mr. Whitfield affirmatively waived his right to testify in the guilt phase, when doing so would have allowed the State to impeach his testimony with evidence of prior crimes. It became just as clear to me, however, that Mr. Whitfield vigorously attempted to exercise his right to testify at the penalty phase, by asking the judge if he could speak to the jury.

During the penalty phase, the jury has already found the defendant guilty. The penalty phase is the defendant's opportunity to provide mitigating evidence and attempt to humanize himself before the jury, to avoid the sentence of death. After the penalty phase began, Mr. Whitfield asked if he could talk on his own behalf. Mr. Whitfield's counsel then asked to make a record of what Mr. Whitfield would say, but the trial judge ignored this and told Mr. Whitfield he could not "give a speech" to the jury and could only address the jury if his lawyer called him as a witness. The trial judge then shifted the focus from Mr. Whitfield's right to testify to his separate right of allocution, and assured Mr. Whitfield that before he imposed a sentence, Mr. Whitfield would be permitted to talk to the judge directly. (Allocution is an unsworn statement from a convicted defendant to the sentencing judge in which the defendant can ask for mercy, explain his conduct, apologize for the crime, or say anything else in an effort to lessen the impending sentence. By the time of allocution, however, the jury has already reached a verdict in the penalty phase, so speaking to the judge after the jury returns its verdict is not the same as testifying before the jury.)

Despite Mr. Whitfield's expressed desire to testify during the penalty phase, his attorney did not call him to the witness stand. As the proceeding ended, the judge did not question Mr. Whitfield about it or inform him of his continuing right to testify, but instead merely asked Mr. Whitfield's attorney if all the evidence was concluded. She responded that Mr. Whitfield was reserving his right to allocution before the court at sentencing. After closing arguments were made, the judge sent the jury out to consider its verdict in the penalty phase. At that point, Mr. Whitfield realized what was happening and rose from his chair and requested to address the jury. The trial judge ignored this request and adjourned the case, reconvening only after the jury reported that it had deadlocked with an eleven-to-one vote in favor of life.

After Mr. Whitfield was convicted, the trial judge conducted a hearing on Mr. Whitfield's motion for a new trial based on newly discovered evidence and motion for imposition of a life sentence. At one point in this hearing, Mr. Whitfield was given the opportunity to address the judge. He did so at length, for nineteen pages of transcript, and spoke with powerful language of his difficult life history and circumstances including brain damage from several head injuries, his love for his father, his reputation in the community as "Uncle Joe," a person neighborhood children came to for advice, and the effect his execution would have on his daughter, whose mother had been murdered in 1988. After reading the transcript of Mr. Whitfield's words, I thought that if the jurors had heard him speak on his own behalf, there was a good chance the one hold-out juror would have voted for life. Because Mr. Whitfield's right to testify at the penalty phase had been violated, I issued a writ of habeas corpus that vacated the death sentence and ordered the State of Missouri to elect whether to resentence Mr. Whitfield to life in prison without parole, or provide him a new penalty phase trial. (There was no basis to vacate the conviction itself, only the sentence of death.)

Many people don't like the fact that on occasion, convicted criminals, including murderers, can have a verdict or sentence overturned on what they consider to be a legal technicality. I would tell people that violations of fundamental constitutional rights are not legal technicalities at all. Rather, they are some of the most basic and important rights that any of us as American citizens possess. It just so happens that criminal cases are where the rubber meets the road for constitutional purposes, where the boundaries of our fundamental constitutional rights are most often tested and preserved for all of us. People who are accused of crimes, some of whom are innocent, are placed in a position where they need to exercise the rights guaranteed by the Constitution more than the rest of us tend to do on a daily basis. In doing so, they defend and preserve the constitutional rights that protect us, no matter who we are.

The State of Missouri appealed my decision to the Eighth Circuit Court of Appeals. The Eighth Circuit affirmed my denial of the majority of Mr. Whitfield's claims, but reversed my grant of a writ of habeas corpus by a vote of two to one in April 2003. My focus here is on the dissent written by the late Judge Gerald Heaney. Judge Heaney discussed the fundamental nature of the right to testify, and agreed that Mr. Whitfield unequivocally invoked his right to testify. He concluded that Mr. Whitfield's "obvious invocations of his right to testify were not honored by the trial court; and for the majority to hold otherwise stretches the governing law and the facts of this case beyond their elasticity." Judge Heaney reasoned that given Mr. Whitfield's affecting speech and the jury's deadlock at eleven-to-one in favor of life, if Mr. Whitfield had been able to present his personal testimony, he may well have changed the mind of the hold-out juror.

Judge Heaney concluded that Mr. Whitfield's "most sacred constitutional right" had been violated, and strongly disagreed with the majority opinion:

Joseph Whitfield repeatedly asked the trial court to honor one request: allow him to testify on his own behalf. He attempted to exercise this most sacred constitutional right at least twice; nonetheless, the majority inexplicably concludes that, despite Whitfield's two emphatic requests to speak, he somehow waived the very right he was seeking to exercise. The creation of such a legal fiction has no place in a case where the defendant's life hangs in the balance. I agree with the district court that Whitfield was denied his right to testify at the penalty phase of his capital trial, and that his counsel rendered ineffective assistance by failing to call him as a witness. Accordingly, I dissent.

Whitfield v. Bowersox, 324 F.3d 1009, 1024 (8th Cir. 2003) (Heaney, J., dissenting).

I was disappointed the Eighth Circuit majority did not see the case as I did, but took some consolation in Judge Heaney's agreement that Mr. Whitfield's fundamental constitutional right to testify in his own behalf had been violated. As a result of the decision, I would be required to vacate the writ of habeas corpus, which would serve to reimpose Mr. Whitfield's death sentence.

Before the case could come back to me, however, Mr. Whitfield filed petitions for rehearing by the three-judge Eighth Circuit panel that decided the case and by the entire Eighth Circuit en banc. While the petitions for rehearing were pending, the Missouri Supreme Court issued a decision that made the federal habeas case irrelevant and moot. In September 2002, Mr. Whitfield's attorneys had filed a motion with the Missouri Supreme Court arguing that the Missouri statute under which the trial judge sentenced Mr. Whitfield to death was unconstitutional as a result of the U.S. Supreme Court's recent decision in *Ring v. Arizona*. The *Ring* case held that capital defendants are entitled to have a jury make any factual determinations on which their eligibility for the death penalty is based. Mr. Whitfield argued that after the jury was unable to agree on his punishment, the trial judge made his own factual determinations on which the death sentence was based, and this violated the requirements of *Ring*. In June 2003, the Missouri Supreme Court agreed and ruled that Mr. Whitfield's death sentence must be set aside, and resentenced Mr. Whitfield to life imprisonment without possibility of parole. The case was over. As a result, everything I had done in Mr. Whitfield's federal habeas case became meaningless, except that it kept him alive long enough for *Ring* to be decided and the Missouri Supreme Court to act. I felt that justice was served in the case.

CHAPTER SIX

The Federal Probation Office and
Hope for Ex-Offenders

I've said before, one of my concerns about the very long prison sentences meted out to drug offenders in federal court is that at some point the vast majority of these offenders will be released. Some will be angry after their years of confinement, and may be released with more criminal knowledge and intent than they had when first incarcerated. This is not true of all ex-offenders, of course. Many desperately want to turn their lives around. Even those with the best intentions, however, often have great difficulty in being able to successfully re-enter society, particularly if they didn't finish high school or never held a legitimate job prior to being incarcerated.

In reviewing over a thousand presentence investigation reports during my first eighteen years on the federal bench, I was struck by the fact that the vast majority of criminal defendants had little opportunity and support in their lives prior to entering prison. Most did not finish high school, let alone higher education, many came from broken families and had little familial support and guidance growing up, including parents in prison or addicted to drugs, some had drug or alcohol addictions of their own, others had mental illness, and few had legitimate employment. When released from prison, many of these men and women will be joining thousands of ex-offenders who already live in the St. Louis area. Every one of us has a stake in seeing that these individuals become healthy, law-abiding neighbors.

Many offenders have a structured existence for the first time in their lives while in federal prison. There, they can take advantage of available programs, in some cases by learning to read, write and perform basic math, while others obtain a GED or even earn college credits. Federal prisoners can participate in intensive substance abuse treatment programs and are able to attend a variety of classes, including occupational and vocational training to learn needed job skills such as welding, carpentry or construction, and classes teaching life skills such as parenting, anger management and finance. Many offenders have truly been able to better themselves while incarcerated, such as Ruth Kane did.

People are often critical of inmates obtaining education while in prison, especially college credits. I hear time and again that prisoners should be serving their sentences and not allowed to do anything else. There is a time and place for punishment, but educational opportunities, even college credits, pay off dividends in the end. We all benefit when inmates are equipped to find jobs when they are released.

After offenders are released, however, they often struggle and fail for lack of support and opportunity. Many do return to crime and prison. Ex-offenders who want to get a job may lack such fundamentals as appropriate clothing for a job interview, the skills necessary to successfully navigate the interview process, or transportation to get to an interview or job. Also, many businesses will not consider hiring a person who has been convicted of a felony.

In 1994, the U.S. Justice Department conducted the largest research project ever on recidivism by tracking 272,111 individuals released from prison for three years. The study showed discouraging results. Of those released:

- 29.9% were rearrested for a felony or serious misdemeanor within six months;
- 44.1% were rearrested within one year;
- 67.5% were rearrested within three years.

Nationally, an unemployed ex-offender is four times more likely to have his supervision revoked than one who is employed. Unemployment and recidivism go hand in hand. In July 2000, the unemployment rate in the St. Louis area was 3.6%. At that time, the unemployment rate of ex-offenders on federal supervision in the Eastern District of Missouri was 12.1%, or more than three times higher than the community rate. Today, the percentages in the Eastern District of Missouri are much different as a result of innovative programs implemented here, and this is despite the fact that unemployment rates in general have increased significantly in recent years.

Pioneering work done by the U.S. Probation Office in the Eastern District of Missouri under the leadership of its Chief, Douglas Burris, gives me hope that ex-offenders will have a better chance to return to the community as productive members, rather than returning to prison. I consider our district's Probation Office to be the flagship of our federal courthouse. Traditionally, the focus of federal probation offices has been on catching ex-offenders when they violate some aspect of their supervised release conditions, such as by using alcohol or drugs, and getting their supervision revoked and the person returned to prison. Doug Burris has radically changed the attitude in the Federal Probation Office in St. Louis. The focus now is to help ex-offenders make a successful return to society.

I've referred to Probation Officers as being "the hardest working act in show business," the phrase employed to describe the late James Brown and his band. The vast majority of Probation Officers in this district have advanced degrees, including several with law degrees, and they put their skills and expertise to good use in performing their many duties. One of their key duties is the preparation of presentence investigation reports (PSR) for sentencings. In the PSR, Probation Officers make all of the initial calculations of sentencing guideline ranges, and consult with the AUSAs and defense attorneys about any objections or modifications to those calculations before sending the final report to the judge and the parties. (The PSR is also known as the "black book," after the black three-ring binder in which it is delivered to judges' chambers.) The PSR is a lengthy document that contains all the pertinent information about the charged offense, other relevant conduct, the defendant's prior criminal record, and a detailed family, medical and educational history. It is a comprehensive report on the individual to be sentenced. The Probation Officer who prepared the PSR will be in the courtroom at sentencing if any question arises about anything in the report. Probation Officers also spend much of their time supervising and actively assisting their clients, offenders who have been sentenced to probation or who have served their jail time and are on supervised release. This includes visiting their clients where they live and work. Probation Officers have a difficult job that can be dangerous, and they do it admirably. I have great respect for them.

Knowing that unemployed ex-offenders are far more likely to return to prison, Chief Burris has made employment a vital part of the Probation Office's re-entry program, and reorganized the entire office to focus on cutting unemployment and helping ex-offenders find productive jobs. Under his leadership, the Probation Office teamed with the U.S. Department of Labor and began offering apprenticeship opportunities to ex-offenders. These training programs can last up to three years, and are geared toward careers that pay living wages, such as welding, sheet metal work, plumbing, auto mechanics and construction. The office collaborated with faith-based organizations to establish successful mentoring programs, training programs and assistance for basic living necessities.

A shocking number of people released from prison leave with only the clothes on their back and no place to live. So the Probation Office established a clothing room and food pantry inside the federal courthouse to assist ex-offenders, and formed relationships with various shelters and other organizations for short-term placement. The Probation Office also created a home-ownership program for ex-offenders called Project Home, which is available to ex-offenders who are employed full-time and are complying with all conditions of their supervision. This program guides ex-offenders through the home buying process, even if credit issues arise. With the help of this program, forty-two ex-offenders have purchased homes.

The Probation Office has established an education program, working with organizations in the City of St. Louis and nearly every county in the district to provide GED testing and training. This program has expanded to include secondary education, such as trade schools and colleges. This program's most notable success story so far is Mr. Clark Porter, an individual removed from his mother's home when he was four years old because the mother could not care for him. Mr. Porter spent the next twelve years in ten foster homes, and was released to the streets at age sixteen. At age seventeen, he robbed a post office, taking $400 in cash and $350 in stamps. Mr. Porter was convicted of this offense and served fifteen years at the federal prison in Marion, Illinois, one of two federal prisons where "the worst of the worst" go. Upon his release, he developed an excellent relationship with his Probation Officers who helped him adapt to the community. Mr. Porter first earned his GED, and then an associate's degree at a local community college. In 2006, this man, who had virtually no guidance growing up, graduated with a bachelor's degree in psychology from Washington University in St. Louis, where he was also employed, and then earned a master's degree in social work. Today, Mr. Porter is employed by the Probation Office. The achievements he has made, with the support of the Probation Office, are remarkable.

Our Probation Office has truly become a full-service resource for ex-offenders. Its Money Smart program helps ex-offenders learn to handle money and avoid predatory lenders, and the Cognitive Skills program helps them learn more effective ways to cope with everyday situations in the community, to avoid negative thinking traps that make it easy to act impulsively or illegally, and to stay away from drugs and alcohol. The Mental Health Resource Team consists of Probation Officers licensed in counseling or social work, who help ex-offenders with mental health issues, including crisis situations that may arise. There are also intensive programs to help ex-offenders with substance abuse issues and to assist former gang members in their efforts to succeed after incarceration.

As a result of the Probation Office's innovative programs, and because employers are giving ex-offenders opportunities, the unemployment rate of ex-offenders under supervision in the Eastern District of Missouri has actually been lower than the entire St. Louis community for the last 72 consecutive months. In January 2013, the ex-offender unemployment rate was 5.9% compared to 7.3% for all of Missouri. In addition, the recidivism rate in this district has decreased significantly. In 1994, the re-arrest rate after three years for those released from prison was 14.9%, a figure much lower than the national average of 67.5%. For the year ending December 31, 2012, however, the re-arrest rate in this district was less than 6.8%, almost a 60% reduction. In addition, 194 ex-offenders were released early from supervision based on their successful re-entry into society, saving the government more than $2,000,000.

These numbers show that ex-offenders want to work, they want to support themselves and their families, they want to prove to themselves and others that they can make it, and they do not want to return to prison. The lower recidivism rates that come from support programs offered by the Probation Office mean less money spent on prisons. Employed ex-offenders become taxpayers, too. But most important, the successful integration of ex-offenders back into society results in stronger families and safer communities.

The Federal Probation Office in St. Louis has been so successful in helping ex-offenders succeed that many others look to it as a model for setting up similar programs. Pat Nolan, the Vice President of Prison Fellowship and author of the book *When Prisoners Return*, has remarked, "Of all the re-entry efforts across the nation, St. Louis is clearly the best." Because of the successes of the re-entry programs, our Probation Office representatives have been invited to the White House on eight occasions, four under President George W. Bush and four under President Barack Obama. Notably, in April 2008, Chief Burris was the only employee of the federal judiciary invited to the White House for the President's signing of the Second Chance Act, the most comprehensive bill ever passed by Congress aimed at reducing recidivism through proactive services for ex-offenders.

The St. Louis Federal Probation Office and its leader, Douglas Burris, have demonstrated that when government and community work together, and the focus for ex-offenders is on providing support and opportunity, everyone benefits. I am extremely proud that our Probation

Office is leading the way in developing new ideas to help ex-offenders make a successful return to society. The office's success is a bright spot in the otherwise bleak landscape of incarceration, and offers hope that the many thousands still incarcerated may have a real opportunity to break the cycle of poverty and violence upon their release.

CHAPTER SEVEN

Civil Cases

While I believe that criminal cases and the constitutional issues they raise are at the core of the judicial system, I don't mean to lessen the importance of civil cases. Civil cases are critical to the litigants involved and to society as a whole, because the civil justice system provides a means to peacefully resolve disputes and provide a remedy for those who have been wronged or injured. To me, however, civil cases can sometimes pale in comparison to criminal cases because in so many civil cases, especially commercial disputes, only money is at stake, not a person's life or liberty. The two cannot be equated.

Upon becoming a federal judge, I realized that many of the civil cases filed in federal court were quite different from those filed in state court. When I took the federal bench in 1994, the majority of cases were for employment discrimination, prisoner civil rights, state and federal prisoner habeas corpus cases, and other types of civil rights cases. There were also cases based on complex federal statutes, such as ERISA (the Employee Retirement Income and Security Act), patent, labor, antitrust and telecommunication laws, and appeals from the bankruptcy court. I didn't have much experience with those kinds of cases, and it was a challenge to quickly get up to speed on the law. Beginning in 2007, as a result of changes in both state and federal law, fewer employment discrimination cases are being filed in federal court and more in state court, and the number of prisoner civil rights cases has dropped dramatically. As a result of the economy, there has been a recent increase in federal Fair Debt Collection Practices Act cases and appeals from the denial of social security disability benefits. My current caseload consists of the kinds of cases mentioned above in addition to a varied mixture of everything from insurance disputes, personal injury cases and copyright infringement to breach of contract matters. I generally find there is something new and something to learn every day.

I've had the privilege and responsibility of handling over 4,100 civil cases in federal court to date. There is no way to estimate how many orders I've written or cases I've decided by written opinion, but they are legion. Many times I've written opinions granting summary judgment where I felt sympathy for the plaintiff, but found there was no genuine issue of material fact that remained to require a trial by jury. If a factual dispute exists, however, the facts are to be viewed in the light most favorable to the party seeking to avoid summary judgment, often the plaintiff. If there is an issue of fact that remains to be decided, a plaintiff deserves his or her day in court. It is up to the jury to decide witness credibility, to weigh the evidence, and to draw inferences from the facts. That is not up to me. Defense counsel should be held to their burden of proof in seeking summary judgment, and I will not issue summary judgment in favor of a defendant in a close case. In my years as a federal judge, I've read thousands of Eighth Circuit Court of Appeals opinions concerning summary judgments entered by other district judges. I often joke that my job is to dispose of cases, but in truth I think that perhaps I dispose of fewer cases on summary judgment than some others.

I'm proud that my decisions in civil cases have not been reversed by the Eighth Circuit very often. In April 2010, at a ceremony where I received an award from the American College of Trial Lawyers marking my transition to senior status, I was very honored by Eighth Circuit Chief Judge William J. Riley's remark that my civil opinions are some of the best he's ever seen.

In state court I would receive a civil case on the morning it was ready for trial, and scramble to become familiar with it. In federal court, I have the luxury of receiving a case the day it is filed, in most instances, and managing its progress from beginning to end. Even with the additional time to know and understand a case, some matters can present a challenge. For me, this was particularly true of cases alleging patent infringement. In those cases, the judge is required to determine, as a matter of law, what the language in the patent document itself means. This can be surprisingly difficult even in cases with relatively simple inventions such as stacking wire shelves, a continuous pinless extruded aluminum door hinge, an orthodontic bracket, or "a pet grooming tool, for use with a furry pet," all of which were patent cases of mine.

The task became very daunting when I had to determine what complex scientific, engineering or biomedical language meant in a case involving a patented item such as a jet engine, a "Lentiviral LTR-deleted Vector," a "Sitostanol Formulation with Emulsifier to Reduce Cholesterol Absorption and Method for Preparing and Use of Same" or, in one particularly challenging case, patents for "nucleic acids for diagnosing and modeling Alzheimer's disease," "amyloid precursor protein in Alzheimer's disease," and "isolated cell comprising HAPP 670/671 DNAS sequences." (I have to admit I was not unhappy when that case settled after an evidentiary hearing on the patent claims but before I was required to issue a decision.) To my knowledge, none of my decisions in patent cases were reversed by the Federal Circuit Court of Appeals, which hears all patent appeals. I decided to quit while I was ahead, and I no longer hear patent cases on senior status.

Lawyers will sometimes say they have "bathtub brain." What they mean by this is that their minds become filled with the facts and law of a particular case and they become experts on the subject matter at issue, but when the case is over, they pull the plug and it all goes down the drain and is largely forgotten. The same is true of me as a judge. Some of the civil cases do remain in my mind because they were difficult to resolve, the law was particularly interesting, or the facts were compelling. Others are memorable because they were simply ludicrous, such as the suit under the Racketeer Influenced and Corrupt Organizations Act seeking $10 million in damages and $800 million in punitive damages based on a claim that a copy machine was poorly designed and built to require frequent and costly drum cartridge changes. The following are some of the federal civil cases that have stayed with me over the years.

Nunley v. Ethel Hedgeman Lyle Academy
Sexual Harassment

One memorable case involved three female plaintiffs who worked as security guards and office administrative personnel at Ethel Hedgeman Lyle Academy, which was a charter school in St. Louis. They sued the Academy for allegedly allowing its Executive Director to subject them to a sexually hostile environment. All three plaintiffs testified at an evidentiary hearing, and the harassment and abuse they testified to at the hands of the director, the highest ranking official at the Academy at the time, was truly harrowing. It was unbelievable to me then, as it is now, that such a work place could exist. When the plaintiffs complained about the sexual harassment, the director allegedly threatened to place one woman on probation, orchestrated the firing of another, and unilaterally changed the third plaintiff's work schedule so that she'd be working on the weekends when he could more easily sexually harass her.

Although the plaintiffs were extremely sympathetic and they likely had a meritorious case, they had sued the wrong party. Unbeknownst to the plaintiffs, the director was not an employee of Ethel Hedgeman Lyle Academy; instead he was an employee of the Academy's management company, Imagine Schools. The plaintiffs should have sued Imagine Schools, but did not realize they had sued the wrong party for more than a year. By the time they realized the mistake, it was too late. The deadline for filing suit against Imagine Schools had passed.

It seemed these plaintiffs who allegedly suffered extreme sexual harassment and abuse were out of luck. Because of the rules of procedure in federal court, however, if Imagine Schools knew of the plaintiffs' suit against Ethel Hedgeman Lyle Academy within four months of its filing, and also knew that the case should have been brought against Imagine Schools, the case would be able to proceed against Imagine Schools. There was enough information in the record of the case to show that Imagine Schools knew of the plaintiffs' case against Ethel Hedgeman Lyle Academy shortly after it was filed. Imagine Schools, however, denied knowledge of the case. That denial still surprises me. In any event, the plaintiffs quickly pointed to the irrefutable evidence that

Imagine Schools knew of their case, and shortly thereafter the parties settled.

This case sticks with me largely because of the emotional and graphic testimony of the women at the evidentiary hearing regarding the alleged conduct. Also, although I do not know the details of the settlement with Imagine Schools, I know that because Imagine Schools was a larger employer than the Academy, the plaintiffs were entitled to a much larger maximum damage award under the law than they would have been if their suit had continued against the Academy. I also feel confident the plaintiffs would have never collected on any judgment they received against the Academy, as it was shut down shortly after plaintiffs discovered they'd sued the wrong entity. It was so far behind on paying its bills that state regulators feared for the welfare of its students.

Biomedical Systems Corp. v. GE Marquette Medical Systems, Inc.
Breach of Contract

In my experience, juries in federal court in the Eastern District of Missouri are more conservative and less likely to return large verdicts than juries in state court, though there are exceptions. The largest verdict ever returned by one of my juries in federal court was in a complex breach of contract and fraud case. The plaintiff and defendant companies entered into a contract that required the defendant to obtain something known as "510(k)" premarket notification clearance from the U.S. Food and Drug Administration for a home uterine-activity monitor for use by women with full-term pregnancies, that was based on technology developed by the plaintiff. This process was expected to take ninety days. Instead, the defendant asked the FDA to reclassify the monitor from one class of regulated devices to another class of regulated devices, which took three and a half years. Two and a half years after the contract was signed, the plaintiff sued seeking damages of $135 million. I denied the defendant's summary judgment motion and the case proceeded to trial. The counsel tables in the courtroom were full to overflowing, as both sides had multiple attorneys. It was a hotly contested case that lasted sixteen days, one of my longer jury trials. Ultimately, the jury decided in the plaintiff's favor on the breach of contract claim and awarded it $75 million dollars, which was affirmed on appeal.

While I remember the large verdict, my clerk Michele Crayton remembers that one day after I had recessed trial for the day and left the courtroom, two attorneys who had been having heated exchanges in front of the jury all day began to exchange words with each other. The words were about to turn into action as the lawyers suddenly got in each other's faces, and one of their paralegals yelled for them to stop. Michele was astounded and certain she was going to witness a lawyer fistfight in the courtroom. The situation escalated so quickly she abandoned her initial idea of summoning a court security officer and instead called out in a commanding voice, "Counsel! Counsel! You've gotta take that out of here!" Fortunately, her words got through to them and they backed apart. While verbal fisticuffs may be a litigator's stock in trade, the physical variety are generally not.

Southwestern Bell Telephone, L.P. v.
Missouri Public Service Commission
Telecommunications

The most intellectually challenging decision I've made as a federal judge was in a case under the Federal Telecommunications Act of 1996. Southwestern Bell, which under the Telecommunications Act is classified as an "incumbent local exchange telephone carrier," brought an action against the Missouri state public utility commission and a number of its competitors seeking declaratory and injunctive relief. Bell contended that an order of the utility commission required it to provide its competitors access to Bell's telecommunications network that went well beyond the access authorized by Federal Communications Commission regulations.

The case raised complex legal issues on which there were very few court decisions to offer guidance, and the underlying telecommunications technology was complicated and difficult to understand. The parties filed lengthy cross-motions for summary judgment that addressed the legal issues as well as the underlying telecommunications technology, and my review included the 2,075 page arbitrator's report. It was very difficult and time consuming, and I ended up issuing a 56 page opinion that upheld some but not all of the public service commission's order. I felt good about the opinion, but on rereading it seems largely incomprehensible. This is one of those cases where I have to plead bathtub brain. I was glad the decision was affirmed by the court of appeals, because I sure didn't want to have to take a second shot at it.

Pottgen v. Missouri High School Athletic Activities Association
Americans With Disabilities Act

I fondly remember one of my earliest rulings in a federal civil case, decided in April 1994, even though it was reversed by the court of appeals. The plaintiff, Edward Pottgen, was a nineteen-year-old high school senior who had repeated two grades in elementary school because of a learning disability. Because Mr. Pottgen turned nineteen before his senior year in high school, a Missouri State High School Activities Association ("MSHSAA") rule barred him from playing baseball during his senior year. Under the rule, Mr. Pottgen was thirty-five days too old to play. His lawsuit asserted that the rule barring students over age nineteen from participating in interscholastic competition violated Section 504 of the Rehabilitation Act and the Americans with Disabilities Act (ADA), and asked that he be permitted to play.

After holding a two-day evidentiary hearing, I issued a decision granting a preliminary injunction to prohibit the MSHSAA from enforcing its age rule against him. I found that Mr. Pottgen's mother, who had died three years prior, had used his participation in school sports, particularly baseball, as motivation to help him overcome his learning disability, and that his grades and attitude in school improved as a result of his participation in interscholastic sports. Mr. Pottgen had not been diagnosed to obtain the special educational services he needed for academic success until after he had been held back twice, and he had made steady improvement since receiving special services. Addressing some of the MSHSAA's arguments, I found that Mr. Pottgen would not exceed the limit of eight semesters of participation if allowed to play, he was not physically advanced for his age, and he was not in high school any longer than any other student in the high school grades. In addition, Mr. Pottgen had been contacted by junior colleges as a result of his baseball skills, he could not afford to attend college without some form of financial assistance, and his chances of being offered a junior college athletic scholarship would be greatly reduced if he did not play baseball during his senior year.

Ultimately, I concluded that Mr. Pottgen was a "qualified individual with a disability" under the ADA, and that waiver of the age limit was a reasonable accommodation of his disability that would not fundamentally alter the nature of the program provided by MSHSAA. I also concluded that Mr. Pottgen would be irreparably harmed if he was not allowed to play baseball. Several other courts had granted preliminary injunctions to students with disabilities, finding they would suffer irreparable harm if not allowed to compete in interscholastic athletic events after they had been declared ineligible.

After the baseball season had ended, the Eighth Circuit Court of Appeals reversed my grant of injunctive relief. It determined that Mr. Pottgen was not a qualified individual with a disability under the statutes because the age limit was an essential or necessary eligibility requirement that lessens the competitive advantage of using older players and discourages redshirting. The court of appeals also determined that waiver of the age limit would be unreasonable because it would alter the fundamental nature of the MSHSAA program. While I can't dispute the Eighth Circuit's decision, I believed at the time that my decision was correct under the law and the facts, and I'm glad Mr. Pottgen was able to play baseball during his senior year of high school. I don't know what happened to Mr. Pottgen after that, but I've always remembered him and hoped things went well for him.

Some years later, the U.S. Supreme Court held in a case called *PGA Tour, Inc. v. Martin*, 532 U.S. 661 (2001), that allowing disabled professional golfer Casey Martin to use a golf cart, despite the walking requirement that applied to the PGA's tours, was not a modification that would fundamentally alter the nature of those events, and was required by the ADA. I wondered if the result in *Pottgen* might have been different had the Supreme Court's *Martin* decision been available as precedent at the time.

Stoneridge Investment Partners LLC v. Charter Communications, Inc.
Securities Fraud

I had only one occasion to handle a multi-district litigation ("MDL") case, but it was a notable case. An MDL is a case in which multiple lawsuits concerning a single subject that have been filed in courts anywhere in the country are consolidated into a single case. The goal of a MDL is to promote judicial efficiency and reduce the parties' litigation costs. My MDL consisted of fourteen class-action and shareholder derivative suits filed against cable television provider Charter Communications in 2002, and was known as *Stoneridge*. The case received more national legal media attention than any other civil case I ever had, as much interest focused on the appeals of a decision I made that went all the way to the U.S. Supreme Court.

The *Stoneridge* plaintiffs challenged Charter's accounting practices with respect to how it counted subscribers. The complaint alleged that Charter and other defendants, including some of Charter's officers and its accounting firm, Arthur Andersen LLP, engaged in a fraudulent scheme to artificially boost Charter's customer base and its reported financial results by inflating its subscriber numbers in 2001 by over 100,000 customers, failing to disconnect customers whose accounts were past due, and delaying disconnect requests by customers, in order to meet stock analysts' forecasts for subscriber growth and to portray itself to investors as a growing company.

The plaintiffs also alleged that Charter had entered into sham agreements with two suppliers of digital set-top cable converter boxes to inflate its operating cash flow for the fourth quarter of 2000. (A digital set-top box was a unit typically placed on top of a television set to enable the customer to access digital cable television and other digital services. In 2000, this was relatively new equipment.) Under these alleged sham agreements, Charter would pay the suppliers an extra $20 for each set-top box, and then the suppliers would repay that same amount to Charter in the form of "advertising." Although these agreements could have no legitimate effect on Charter's operating cash flow, the plaintiffs alleged Charter used the transactions to artificially and significantly inflate its cash flow by treating the "advertising payments" as revenues for accounting purposes, when in fact they were simply the return of Charter's own money. The plaintiffs alleged that Charter overpaid the set-top box suppliers by about $17 million in 2000 and received the same amount back, and overstated its 2000 revenue by $17 million.

In addition to the civil lawsuits, there was a federal criminal indictment against two of Charter's officers, and the Securities and Exchange Commission issued a cease-and-desist order against Charter. Eventually, Charter, some of its officers, and accounting firm Arthur Andersen LLP agreed to settle the *Stoneridge* plaintiffs' claims for $146 million without admitting any wrongdoing, and I approved that settlement in June 2005.

The *Stoneridge* plaintiffs also sued the set-top box suppliers, Scientific-Atlanta, Inc. and Motorola, Inc., alleging they agreed to the sham transactions with Charter knowingly or recklessly disregarding that Charter intended to fraudulently inflate its reported results, and knowing that stock analysts would be relying on those reported results in making their recommendations. The plaintiffs alleged that by participating in the sham agreements, Scientific-Atlanta and Motorola violated federal securities laws by making materially misleading statements to Charter investors.

Scientific-Atlanta and Motorola did not participate in Charter's settlement with the *Stoneridge* plaintiffs, and instead filed a motion to dismiss the claims against them. I granted the motion to dismiss in October 2004, concluding the plaintiffs' claims against these defendants were barred by a 1994 Supreme Court decision which held that secondary actors were not liable under the federal securities laws for "aiding and abetting" a federal securities law violation, unless they themselves made a false or misleading statement or omission that they knew or should have known would reach potential investors. There were no factual allegations in the *Stoneridge* plaintiffs' complaint that Scientific-Atlanta or Motorola had created, participated in, or even knew about Charter's accounting treatment, that they made any public representations about Charter, or that any Charter investor relied on anything Scientific-Atlanta or Motorola said. As a result, I concluded these defendants could not have violated federal securities laws by virtue of engaging in a business enterprise with Charter, which was the entity alleged to have actually made the false and misleading statements at issue.

The plaintiffs appealed my decision dismissing their claims against Scientific-Atlanta and Motorola to the Eighth Circuit Court of Appeals, which affirmed the dismissal in March 2006. The plaintiffs then appealed to the U.S. Supreme Court, which granted a writ of certiorari and agreed to hear the case. The *National Law Journal* described *Stoneridge* as "one of the most important securities cases in a generation," because it addressed the question, "Who, besides the chief actor in a securities fraud, can be sued in private securities litigation?" and would resolve a conflict in rulings among several circuit courts of appeal. The *Wall Street Journal* reported that an unusually high number of "friend of the court" briefs were filed in the Supreme Court on both sides of the *Stoneridge* case by a "list of high-powered attorneys, law professors and former government officials . . . [that] reads like a who's who in securities law." Much interest was focused on *Stoneridge* because the Supreme Court's anticipated decision was viewed as likely to affect the potential securities law liability of those involved in the corporate scandal involving the collapse of Enron Corporation, which had sustained itself by means of systematic accounting fraud and filed for bankruptcy in 2001. Interestingly, the Arthur Andersen accounting firm was Enron's independent auditor as well as Charter's.

The Supreme Court affirmed the Eighth Circuit's *Stoneridge* opinion in a 5-3 decision authored by Justice Anthony M. Kennedy on January 15, 2008. The *New York Times* characterized the Supreme Court's decision as "its most important securities fraud case in years," and other major media sources also commented on the decision, including the *Wall*

Street Journal, Forbes and *Business Week.* SCOTUSblog, an online legal blog, stated that "[t]he Supreme Court, in one of the most important securities law rulings in years, decided Tuesday that fraud claims are not allowed against third parties that did not directly mislead investors but were business partners with those who did." There is even a Wikipedia article about the Supreme Court's *Stoneridge* opinion. It was exciting to have written a decision that turned out to concern an issue of great interest, and to have the decision ultimately affirmed by the Supreme Court was icing on the cake.

Moran v. Clarke
Civil Rights and Recusal

On April 14, 1997, two St. Louis police officers responded to a report of a burglar alarm at an apartment. Inside the apartment, the officers encountered Gregory Bell, a mentally impaired African-American teenager. Bell's impairment prevented him from providing the proper alarm code or explaining to the officers that he lived there. Thinking that Bell was a burglar, the officers attempted to place him under arrest but he resisted. During the ensuing fight, the officers repeatedly struck Bell with metal batons and sprayed him with mace. During the struggle, one of the officers placed an "officer in need of aid" call and numerous officers responded, including Sgt. Thomas Moran, a white man, who had been on duty at a police substation. In the end, Bell was left seriously injured with severe head lacerations and a broken ankle.

Bell's beating caused racial tensions to heighten in the City of St. Louis and much public criticism was directed at the police department. Within three days of the incident, then-Police Chief Ronald Henderson, an African American, publicly apologized for the mistake and promised to take appropriate action if there was any wrongdoing. On April 19, 1997, police officer Barry Greene gave a tape-recorded statement to Chief Henderson and police Internal Affairs officers, in which he stated that he saw Sgt. Moran assault Gregory Bell, while the official police report that had been filed placed Sgt. Moran at the scene only after Bell was outside his home. As a result, the St. Louis Circuit Attorney presented the matter to a grand jury and Sgt. Moran was indicted, charged with assault and conspiracy to hinder prosecution.

Police officials continued to investigate, and Sgt. Moran was ultimately charged by the department's Bureau of Professional Standards with assault, use of excessive force with a police baton, and use of excessive force with mace. A charge of failure to properly exercise his duties as a police sergeant was later added. Sgt. Moran was acquitted of the criminal charges by a jury in May 1998, but the department continued to pursue internal charges against him. An administrative hearing was held on the internal charges in June and July of 1998. The hearing officer recommended to the Board of Police Commissioners that Sgt. Moran be acquitted on the assault and excessive force charges, but that the charge of failure to properly exercise his duties be sustained on the grounds that Sgt. Moran directed another officer to file a false report on the Bell beating. The Police Board accepted these recommendations and concluded that Bell was beaten after he had been subdued by police officers, Sgt. Moran was on the scene and was in charge at the time, and therefore Sgt. Moran was guilty of failing to exercise his authority to prevent the beating. The Board sustained Sgt. Moran's earlier suspension without pay and demoted him to patrolman. Officer Moran appealed the Board's decision to the circuit court for the City of St. Louis, which affirmed the Board's action.

In April 1998, Officer Moran filed a federal civil rights lawsuit against eighteen defendants including the five members of the Board, Chief Henderson, and other police officials and officers who were part of the department's Internal Affairs Division. Officer Moran's suit asserted that the defendants solicited false statements against him at a pre-suspension hearing and in grand jury proceedings in violation of his due process rights, conspired to cause his suspension, arrest and prosecution, and maliciously instigated the prosecution against him. The case was randomly assigned to me.

At some point during the pretrial discovery proceedings, Officer Moran's counsel took the deposition of defendant Anne-Marie Clarke, an African-American attorney and President of the Board of Police Commissioners. The attorney asked Ms. Clarke if she knew me, if we were social friends, if I had been to her home, and if she had been to my home and how many times. She responded that we had been in each other's homes several times but not more than ten, over a period of some twenty years. He did not ask Ms. Clarke why or on what occasions those visits took place. Officer Moran's attorney asked Ms. Clarke if I was close personal friends with another member of the Board, to which she responded that we were acquaintances. He also asked Ms. Clarke if she had ever discussed the case with me, which she denied.

Based on these questions and answers, Officer Moran filed a motion for me to recuse myself from the case in September 1999, after I had been presiding over it for almost a year and a half, and two months before the trial was to begin. The motion asserted that I was not impartial because I was a friend of Ms. Clarke, a defendant. I summarily denied the motion without explanation because I thought, given the racially charged nature of the claims, that it was nothing more than an inappropriate eleventh-hour attempt to remove me from the case because of my race.

In addition, the motion for recusal was totally without merit. Ms. Clarke and I had only been in each other's homes for professional or bar-related functions such as an occasion when I hosted a Mound City Bar Association gathering (the Mound City Bar Association is a black bar association based in St. Louis), and we were never in each other's homes as private guests. I did not have a personal relationship with Ms. Clarke beyond that of other attorneys who appear before me, or a personal bias in her favor, and I did not believe my impartiality might reasonably be questioned based on our presence in each other's homes for bar-related or professional functions. In addition, it was significant to me that although Ms. Clarke was sued in the case in both her individual and official capacities, as were all of the Board's members, she was primarily a nominal defendant. Indeed, at trial, Officer Moran did not even call Ms. Clarke to the stand as a witness. Under those circumstances, my acquaintance with her seemed of even less importance. The only noteworthy thing we otherwise had in common was that we were both African Americans in the St. Louis legal community.

In November 1999, two months after I denied Officer Moran's motion to recuse myself, I denied the defendants' motion for summary judgment and ordered that the case proceed to trial. After Officer Moran presented his evidence over a period of three days, the defendants moved for judgment as a matter of law. Although I had earlier denied the defendants' motion for summary judgment, having now heard all of Officer Moran's case, I concluded that he had insufficient evidence to support it and dismissed it. Officer Moran appealed the dismissal and other rulings, including the denial of the motion to recuse myself from the case.

The appeal was heard and the Eighth Circuit reversed, but that decision was vacated and a rehearing by the full Eighth Circuit en banc was held. The court en banc reversed the dismissal of Officer Moran's case by a majority of six to four, and remanded the case to me for further proceedings and to "revisit and more thoroughly consider and respond to Moran's recusal request." The Eighth Circuit stated that it was "troubled" by the record of a social relationship between me and Ms. Clarke, as "[t]he image of one sitting in judgment over a friend's affairs would likely cause the average person in the street to pause. That the judge and Clarke enjoyed a friendship of sufficient depth and duration as to warrant several reciprocal visits to one another's homes only exacerbates the problem. We find particularly worrisome the district court's failure to disclose this conflict himself[.]" *Moran v. Clarke*, 296 F.3d 638, 649 (8th Cir. 2002).

I felt that the Eighth Circuit majority's opinion unfairly excoriated me for refusing to recuse myself from the case and, in doing so, called into question my reputation and impartiality. The opinion assumed facts that were not in the record and were incorrect: that the attorney and I were personal friends, that we had made "several reciprocal visits" to each other's homes as if we were personal friends, and that the matter presented a conflict of interest that I should have disclosed. I viewed the Eighth Circuit's strong implication questioning my impartiality in the case as disrespectful. The manner in which the Eighth Circuit chose to address the issue unnecessarily trod on a fellow Article III Judge. The case was being reversed on other grounds; why was it necessary to castigate me? Justice Breyer once wrote, "[T]he cardinal principle of judicial restraint is that if it is not necessary to decide more, it is necessary not to decide more." All the court of appeals had to do was direct me to revisit recusal on remand. It was obvious all the relevant facts were not known in the case, but the Eighth Circuit did not hesitate to decide that there was an actual conflict on my part. Had the Court's majority expressed its concerns and then allowed me to set out the relevant facts before it assumed the worst, unnecessary and wrongful damage to my reputation would have been avoided.

When I received the case back following the remand, I wrote an opinion that set out the facts relevant to the issue of recusal and vigorously responded to the Eighth Circuit's accusations:

> The majority assumes a conflict exists, but the facts show otherwise. Neither Clarke nor the undersigned have ever been in each other's homes on a personal, family or "reciprocal" basis. Clarke was last present in the undersigned's home eight years ago in 1994, when I permitted the Mound City Bar Association to host a reception for a candidate running for the presidency of the National Bar Association. Approximately one hundred people attended the event in my home, almost all of whom were members of the bar. Between 1987 and 1993, the undersigned was present in Clarke's home on three occasions. The first occasion was a Missouri Bar Association reception in conjunction with the annual Missouri Bar Conference. The second was a Mound City Bar Association social event. The third was a birthday party for Clarke's husband, who had been president of the St. Louis Board of Education. At each of these gatherings, there were between one to two hundred guests, most of whom were members of the bar or public officials.
>
> Between 1977 and 1978, Clarke and the undersigned were present in each other's homes two to three times as part of a group meeting of approximately half a dozen people attempting to plan and organize an effort to

encourage young African-American professionals in St. Louis to meet, network and socialize. Subsequently, during this same period of time, Clarke was present in the undersigned's home for such a social gathering attended by more than one hundred people. This court's relationship with Clarke was based on our being members of the bar and of the same small generation of African-American attorneys in St. Louis, rather than on personal matters.

Moran v. Clarke, No. 4:98-CV-556 CAS, 213 F. Supp. 2d 1067, 1070-71 (E.D. Mo. 2002). (A copy of the full opinion is set out in the Appendix.)

I concluded by stating that while these facts showed no actual conflict had ever existed, after lengthy consideration I felt compelled to recuse myself from the case because of the way in which the recusal issue had been handled. I could have added that it was not surprising Ms. Clarke and I had been in each other's homes. African-American bar and other professional and social groups have often hosted and attended meetings in their members' homes, as opposed to hotels, restaurants and clubs, where we historically have not been welcome. It did not occur to me that I needed to explain that fact. No more than other attorneys might need to explain why they met over lunch at the Missouri Athletic Club, their country club or an otherwise non-public venue. It had never occurred to me that the mere presence of another attorney in my home could raise an inference that we were personal friends. I felt that the court of appeals majority and I were viewing the facts of the matter across a cultural divide that could not be bridged. It has been said that Supreme Court Justice Thurgood Marshall stated, "Although you can change the law, you cannot change the hearts and minds of men."

In its subsequent opinion, the Eighth Circuit stated that if the facts about the alleged conflict had been in the record at the time of the earlier appeal, it was "certain that [my] denial of the recusal motion would have been summarily affirmed and no remand ordered." Without doubt, I wish I had explained my reasons for denying the recusal motion at the time. Looking back, this was an instance in which recalling Dad's caution, "Watch everything," would have been useful. Nonetheless, I had to question whether the Eighth Circuit majority would have been as willing to make the assumptions it did, including the damning assertion that I sat "in judgment over a friend's affairs," if they had viewed me as a member of their club. Ultimately, the *Moran* case was the event that brought me into maturity as a federal judge. It made me come to grips with the fact that I was appointed to this position for life, absent impeachment, and that I had to carry out my duties in the way I thought was right, regardless of what others might think of me.

Officer Moran's case was retried over a five-day period in April 2004, before a district judge from another judicial district. The jury ruled in favor of the defendants as I had. The jury's verdict was upheld on appeal in 2006.

Chapter Eight

Courtroom Humor

Lawsuits and criminal prosecutions are serious business. Nonetheless, I've always believed that adding some humor to the courtroom helps put everyone at ease and lightens the atmosphere. I generally tell stories to make a point about something pertinent to the proceeding. Here are a few of the stories that lawyers in my courtroom have heard over the years, maybe even more than once.

Make It Easy

Early in my tenure on the federal bench I was conducting informal matters (the morning half hour for brief announcements or requests by attorneys), and attorney Bill Bay was the first to approach the podium. The courtroom was fairly full of attorneys waiting their turn. Bill is a very good and highly respected attorney. He wanted to advise me of the status of his rather complicated case. Bill stated that he had been consulting with the other attorneys in the case, a number of who were present. He then proclaimed, "Judge, I figured out how to make this case easy." After a moment of silence I responded, "For whom?" When no answer came forth I explained to him as follows, "With me sitting up above everyone else, the United States flag by my side, and the Great Seal of our country above me, while wearing a dress, the case must be made easy for me." Bill was left without words and the whole courtroom burst into laughter. I never found out exactly how the case was made easy, but it did resolve itself expeditiously.

The Two Suits

Some prominent New York lawyers representing Yoko Ono in a copyright matter appeared in my courtroom and I welcomed them. I told them this story when it became apparent that the lawyers seemed to think they could take charge of my courtroom:

A couple of months ago another attorney from New York appeared before me. He had gone to his tailor in New York and obtained material for a suit to be tailored by a highly respected tailor here in St. Louis. When he showed the St. Louis tailor the material, the tailor stated that there was enough for two suits. The attorney queried, "How could this be? My New York tailor said it was only enough material for one suit." The St. Louis tailor responded, "Well, you're not as big a lawyer here in St. Louis as you are in New York."

Bob Hope

Several lawyers in a patent infringement case appeared in my court for a hearing on a motion concerning the sworn deposition testimony of some expert witnesses. Before the session started, attorney Tom Douglas, with whom I have had occasion to play golf, mentioned my Lee Trevino rule ("miss it quick") as having similarity to the issue before me. I responded, "Oh, no. It reminds me of when Bob Hope was talking to a bunch of his fellow golfers and one asked, 'Bob, what is your lowest score?' Bob answered, 'Sixty-seven.' Another golfer said, 'Hey Bob, you told me the other day that your lowest score was sixty-nine.' Bob responded, 'Oh, I'm just improving my lie.'"

I'm Not Superman

Richard Pryor told a story about how he took a friend who was suffering from an unknown malady to a voodoo priestess' house. After their arrival, strange and scary events unfolded. Thereupon, Richard admitted, "And that's when I pulled out my knife, 'cause if someone gets hurt around here, I'm not going to be the last one."

That story comes to mind when lawyers will occasionally ask me to do things that are not within my power, or are based on a very dubious legal foundation. When the court of appeals reverses my orders in such a situation, I am the only one found to have erred, not the lawyers. As a judge, I wear a robe, not a cape.

Loose Shoes

It was Monday morning and a jury panel was waiting to come to the courtroom for the scheduled criminal trial. Defense attorney Kevin Curran implored me to delay starting as the defendant's mother was on her way to the courthouse and could more than likely convince her son to accept a favorable plea deal. It transpired just as Kevin predicted. This African-American man took the deal and pleaded guilty. Following the plea, he asked to speak and I consented. The defendant stated that he would not have pleaded guilty were it not for his mother and, besides, the clothes he had on were not his and the shoes were too tight. I responded, "Well, Earl Butz wasn't all wrong." Kevin Curran just about fell out of his chair laughing, while the younger lawyers didn't have a clue. (Earl Butz was the Secretary of Agriculture under President Richard Nixon. He resigned in October 1976 after *Rolling Stone* magazine quoted him as telling a vulgar, racially derogatory joke that said, in part, one of the three things black men wanted was "loose shoes.")

Just Checking

When one of my former law clerks, Keith Grady, appeared in my courtroom on a very complicated case, I made opposing counsel aware of his having clerked for me. I went on to state that Keith was an upstanding, well-respected and trusted member of the Bar, and that he had an outstanding reputation for trustworthiness and honesty. After this parade of accolades, I pointed to the U.S. Marshals and said,

"Nevertheless, as a cautionary measure and for our safety, 'Pat him down.'"

This is an exaggerated take on President Ronald Reagan's admonition, "Trust but verify." I have used this quip after giving accolades about a person to be recognized or introduced. It is a serious ice breaker and a reminder that you should, "Watch everything."

Nothing Less Than a Heavyweight

In cases where the stakes are small and the legal fees will likely exceed any outcome, I generally inquire of the attorneys why the case hasn't settled. When I get an "I don't know" or another vague response, I tell them the following story:

When I was a boy, Dad and my two brothers and I would always watch the *Gillette Friday Night Fights* together on television. It was our guy thing and we thoroughly enjoyed it. This was when TV was free. As an adult after moving to Washington, D.C., I called my father and asked, "Dad, have you seen Sugar Ray Leonard?" My father responded, "Son, I don't watch anything less than a heavyweight."

Don't Try This on Your Own, or Be Sure to Bring a Hatchet

People, generally plaintiffs, who come to court without being represented by a lawyer (pro se) are at a severe disadvantage. I tell them, "Coming to court without a lawyer is like going to a hatchet fight without a hatchet. You could get hurt bad."

You Can't Leave That Here

Occasionally, lawyers seek to withdraw from representing a client in a case where the lawyer has filed the complaint initiating the case on behalf of that same client. I advise them, "What do you think this is, an orphanage? You can't bring this case into my courtroom and just leave it at the door. This is not an orphanage." Attorneys are generally not allowed to withdraw from representing a party absent special circumstances.

Two Bites

Our federal district court in St. Louis has an Internet web page that, among other things, details each judge's individual requirements. Lawyers appearing in a particular judge's courtroom either know or should know that judge's requirements. As to the questioning of witnesses, some judges allow only one round of questioning: direct and cross examination. Any further questions must be first approved by the judge at a bench conference. I, on the other hand, allow two rounds of questioning adding re-direct and re-cross examination. I call it "Two bites at the apple," a description I appropriated from Judge Kenneth Wangelin.

During one trial after the two rounds of questioning had been completed, Charles Kirksey, an excellent trial attorney, rose from his chair and had the temerity to state, "Judge, I have just one more question." I responded, "Mr. Kirksey, that is one too many."

Charles in Charge, or Caution in the Courtroom

Although judges as public servants do not enjoy the luxuries that some private practitioners do, we have control of our courtrooms. As judges, we sit up above everyone else, everyone must stand when we enter the courtroom, we wear robes and are surrounded by the state and American flags. I advised some of my fellow judges that if they allow a lawyer to take control of their courtroom, they are throwing their pay out the window. Among others, attorney Charlie M. Shaw was notorious for taking over a courtroom. In one case he tried before me, he blurted out an objection without even standing, telling his client who was being cross-examined by the prosecutor, "Aww, you don't have to answer that question." I promptly advised him he knew better, that an attorney must stand when making any statement, and what he said was not the proper form of an objection. When he stood and properly phrased his objection, I immediately overruled it and told him, "Sit down."

Some lawyers attempt to overstep the rules and boundaries for their conduct during trial believing that if they go too far, the judge will call them to the bench and address their transgressions out of the jury's hearing. They know that the bell of their conduct before the jury cannot be unrung. I advise lawyers that if they run afoul of obvious rules or otherwise engage in egregious conduct, they will not be called to the bench, but I will cut them in the jury's presence and allow them to bleed right there. I think that this, among other things, makes my trials more civil and brings about more settlements. It also can tend to put a little more stress on the attorneys than some are used to. I expect attorneys to be prepared in the courtroom and not waste the jury's time.

The plaintiff's attorney in a civil case some years ago was woefully ill-prepared and disorganized. His presentation of the plaintiff's evidence was slow and jumbled. The attorney kept asking his witnesses the same questions, over and over again, and his trial exhibits weren't properly marked. When he would refer to an exhibit, its number wouldn't match up with the exhibit list he filed prior to trial, and he would return to counsel table and sort through his voluminous exhibits, trying to find the correct one. This caused a lot of needless delay. During the second day of trial, the attorney announced that the next witness he wanted to call wasn't available. Although I could have called him to task on the spot, I turned on the white noise machine so the jury could not hear and called the attorneys to the bench. I started in on the plaintiff's attorney none too gently, admonishing him for not managing his case well and causing unnecessary delays in the trial. When I was finished, I told the attorney to proceed with his case. As he turned from the bench, he fainted dead away. Fortunately, a nurse was on the jury and began attending to him and I had my deputy clerk call 911 and summon the Marshal for assistance. The sight of a female U.S. Deputy Marshal kicking open the courtroom door and racing in with defibrillator paddles in her hands will always stay with me. The attorney was soon revived and refused any further treatment, and I ended up declaring a mistrial.

Not long before this, a criminal defendant had appeared before me for sentencing. He was represented by Felicia Jones, an Assistant Federal Public Defender. The defendant was a small and slight African-American man, but he was cocky and arrogant when he addressed me prior to the imposition of sentence, arguing that he should not be sent to prison. (As an aside, right before sentence is imposed is not the best time to be smart-mouthed with the judge who is going to sentence you.) I told the defendant that under the mandatory sentencing guidelines, I didn't have much control over his sentence and he was going to have to do the time. I added that since he was such a small guy, he would need to bulk up when he went into prison, for his own safety. As soon as those words left my mouth, he hit the floor, out like a light.

After the second incident, I joked with Michele Crayton that we should put a sign outside the courtroom door reading, "Caution, Appearing in This Courtroom May be Hazardous to Your Health."

The Good Book

I was conducting a sentencing hearing when the federal sentencing guidelines were mandatory. The U.S. Probation Office had prepared the presentence report (the black book) for the Court and parties that contained the mandatory guidelines sentencing range. I was about to sentence the defendant to an agreed-upon mandatory guideline sentence, when he went into an oration about the Bible. First, he quoted the Book of John. Next, the Book of Matthew. Before he could get to his next quote, I told him, "That's all well and good and those are great Books, but unfortunately (while holding up the black book), the only book I have up here is the Book of Numbers, and it looks like I've got to give you a few." Michele had a difficult time maintaining her composure. That was one of the rare times I was able to cause her to lose it.

Justice and Mercy

In the late 1990s our district court had one of its first retreats for the judges to discuss our mission. We had officials from the Federal Judicial

Center in Washington, D.C. leading the discussion. One official raised the question whether we believed the federal courts were delivering justice. I responded saying, "Justice is like beauty, it is in the eye of the beholder. As the famous and well-respected Florida trial lawyer Willie Gary told me, 'Judge, if I ever come before you don't give me justice, give me mercy. That justice is some bad stuff.'" That was the end of our discussion on justice.

I tell attorneys and their clients this story when they are failing or refusing to comply with the Federal Rules or court procedures. I then follow up with my view on justice and their case: "I am here to dispose of cases and if you continue with your behavior, I will sanction you and will disallow your introduction of related evidence, likely hamper or cripple your case, and thereby lead to its prompt disposition."

CHAPTER NINE

Final Thoughts
Charles Will Be Charles (Like Him or Not)

As the late comedian and actor Bernie Mac proclaimed, "I don't care if you don't like me, I like me." And as Oscar Wilde once wrote, "To love oneself is the beginning of a lifelong romance." Charles will be Charles, like him or not.

A friend of mine, Reggie Dickson, has often joked, "If I'm not living on the edge, I'm taking up too much space." When you are working on the "public edge" some people get offended, and I have likely offended my fair share, if not more. This is particularly so when people are the focus of humor. I urge my staff to help keep me in check, telling them, "I think I'm a comedian but I'm a federal judge." (The late Larry Williams, a member of my Saturday golf group, christened me "Judge Chuckles.") Nevertheless, in my heart and head I think humor softens the serious as well as sheds light from a different perspective. To those who I may have offended, please accept my apology.

When my son, Dr. Bryan Shaw, was in his second year of psychiatry residency he called home telling his mother about meeting his fiancée's father. Unbeknownst to them I had picked up the phone, waited to speak and listened. Bryan described his future father-in-law as "a real nice guy, laid back, easy going, not confrontational like Dad." I immediately trumpeted my presence exclaiming, "What are you trying to say about me?" We all laughed, as I had proved his point.

They say the apple doesn't fall far from the tree. My friend Bernard Shaw, now the retired anchor of CNN News, described my father in his eulogy as a "double-barreled dose of candor and bluntness." Not only did I not roll when I fell from that tree, I didn't even oscillate. A plaque on the door leading to my courtroom adapts a phrase from the hymn "Joy to the World" and reads, "Rule with Truth and Grace." I'm good at the truth part but sometimes struggle with the grace part. Retired Congressman Bill Clay once told me, "Keep agitating. The world is worth saving." Oh, I like to agitate, all right, and I like to think it has done the world some good.

I also hope that I have honored the advice of President Bill Clinton, who said, "Remember: Who you are, where you came from, and how you got here." My early life was largely limited to a few city blocks of a segregated African-American neighborhood in north St. Louis. I had very little exposure to the larger world until I moved to Washington, D.C. after college, but in this little incubator I was exposed to a solid work ethic, offered guidance from my supportive parents, and outfitted with a strong suit of perseverance. As to how I got here, I was aided by the help of others and received more than my share of good fortune. As my dear mother frequently told her sons, "Count your blessings." My blessings include but are not limited to my wife, parents, son and daughter-in-law, brothers, friends, staff and colleagues. Thank you one and all for being there and helping me achieve a full and fruitful life. As for my part, I hope I have followed President Barack Obama's directive by making choices that reflected my hopes as opposed to my fears. All in all, the good has outweighed the bad by far. I am truly grateful that good luck and God's hand touched my life.

Bill Clinton also said while reflecting on the short time we are on this earth, "Our job is to live well and as long as we can and to help others do the same. What happens after that and how we are viewed is beyond our control. The river of time carries us all away. All we have is the moment. Whether I made the most of mine was for others to judge."

Appendix

December 1, 1995

Mr. Richard P. Conaboy, Chairman
United States Sentencing Commission
One Columbus Circle, NE
Suite 2-500, South Lobby
Washington, D.C. 20002-4529

Dear Mr. Conaboy:

The issue of whether African-American defendants receive disparate treatment in crack cocaine cases deserves serious examination and reconsideration. Although Congress and President Clinton refused to allow the Sentencing Commission's equalizing recommendations to take effect, the President has urged further study to see whether sentences for crack cocaine should be adjusted downward. It is unfortunate that while echoing the sentiments of the Million Man March criticizing the disproportionate percentage of black men prosecuted and imprisoned for drug offenses, President Clinton declined to veto the legislation maintaining disparate crack sentences.

In 1993, almost 90% of the crack sentences were imposed on blacks while only 4% went to whites. The federal sentencing guidelines and mandatory minimums go easy on large wholesalers of powder cocaine who are overwhelmingly white, yet slam dunk low-level dealers and users who are predominantly black. This is a clear situation of racial inequity where our "War on Drugs" merely slaps enemy officers on the wrist while requiring their foot soldiers to face a firing squad. Furthermore, while the percentage of powder cocaine cases dropped from 42% to 31% of all federal drug cases in 1994, crack cases increased from 15% to 21%. It would appear that the focus of federal prosecution efforts are being directed more toward crack cases and less toward powder cocaine cases. We don't have to ask a constitutional expert whether he or she can see the perverse discrimination, Ray Charles can see it.

Since 1980, the federal prison population has more than tripled. At the end of 1994, black inmates made up more than one-third (35.4%) of that population, while being only 12 percent of the population of the United States. Nearly one-third of the young black men in this country are either in prison, on probation, parole or some form of criminal supervision. Black men in the United States are incarcerated four times greater than in South Africa. Unfortunately, we have more young black men in prison in this country than in college. Only in America.

In 1993, the Department of Justice disclosed that the higher proportion of blacks charged with crack offenses was "[t]he single most important difference accounting for the overall longer sentences imposed on blacks, relative to other racial groups." Crack cocaine sentences clearly have a significant impact not only on the number but the proportion of blacks in prison.

The current drug policy in the country as it relates to crack cocaine is a social and economic failure. This policy not only disproportionately affects and sometimes ruins the lives of the black men involved, but also their families and the community. There is also a fantastic economic cost of putting these young men in prison for inordinately long sentences without any real impact on the "War on Drugs." The real impact is the devastation of young black men's lives who may not benefit from extended imprisonment and thereafter become outcasts from the American taxpaying rolls at a time when the federal budget deficit looms so large. The average cost to confine a federal prisoner as of 1994 was in excess of $21,000 per year. These sentencing policies encourage African Americans to believe that this is a racist society, that it doesn't care about them, so consequently why should they have any respect or concern for it. This situation is unhealthy as these young men "will be back": older and wiser in the ways of crime; perhaps meaner and less caring about society; and perhaps set on seeking some measure of revenge for the inequities visited upon them.

The words above the columns of the United States Supreme Court read: "Equal Justice Under Law," but the disparate treatment between crack and powder cocaine sends the opposite message to our African-American community. The United States Sentencing Commission should undertake a new and comprehensive review of the issues surrounding crack sentences. Bring the experts as well as the general public into the discussion and get all their opinions. The bottom line, I suggest, is a cost/benefit analysis that takes into consideration not only the fact that there is a "War on Drugs" but that we as a country fight fair—we treat all drug offenders the same—that this war will focus on the big fish as opposed to the small fry.

Very truly yours,

Charles A. Shaw

CAS:cdp

cc: President William J. Clinton
    U.S. Attorney General Janet Reno
    Senator Christopher Bond
    Senator John Ashcroft
    Representative Richard A. Gephardt
    Representative William L. Clay

The following opinion from *Moran v. Clarke*, Case No. 4:98-CV-556 CAS (E.D. Mo. Aug. 2, 2002) appears in the format in which it was originally filed in the office of the Clerk of Court of the United States District Court for the Eastern District of Missouri. The opinion is published in West's Federal Reporter Supplement, Second Series, as *Moran v. Clarke*, 213 F. Supp. 2d 1067, 1070-71 (E.D. Mo. 2002), and may also be accessed online via the Westlaw or LEXIS commercial electronic databases, using the same citation.

UNITED STATES DISTRICT COURT
EASTERN DISTRICT OF MISSOURI
EASTERN DIVISION

THOMAS MORAN,   )
)
      Plaintiff,   )
)
      v.   ) No. 4:98-CV-556 CAS
)
ANNE-MARIE CLARKE,   )
et al.,   )
)
     Defendants.   )

MEMORANDUM AND ORDER

This case has been remanded to this court for retrial and, among other things, reconsideration of plaintiff Thomas Moran's recusal request. In preparing to undertake these responsibilities, this court is compelled to examine the facts and proceedings which weigh heavily on the mind of the undersigned.

I.

Factual and Procedural Background

On April 14, 1997, St. Louis police officers mistook a mentally impaired teenager, Gregory Bell, for a burglar in his own home. During his arrest, Bell resisted and was left seriously injured with severe head lacerations and a broken ankle. Within three days, Police Chief Ronald Henderson publicly apologized for the mistake and promised to take appropriate action if there was any wrongdoing. On April 19, 1997, Police Officer Barry Greene gave a tape-recorded statement to Chief Henderson, Major Gregory Hawkins and Captain Paul Nocchiero that he saw Sergeant Moran assault Gregory Bell. The previously submitted police report had placed Moran at the scene only after Bell was outside his home.

Henderson, along with Hawkins, Nocchiero and other officers, took Greene to speak with the prosecuting attorney for the City of St. Louis, Circuit Attorney Dee Joyce-Hayes. Joyce-Hayes subsequently took the matter to a grand jury, which issued an indictment against Moran. During the St. Louis Police Department's continuing investigation, Attorney Richard Barry, who represented Moran, and Attorney Andrew Leonard, who represented other officers, spoke with Chief Henderson. Attorney Barry stated that Chief Henderson said he wanted "the white sergeant." Attorney Leonard stated that he could not recall a racial overtone or any reference to "the white sergeant" during this same conversation. Chief Henderson denied making such a statement.

Moran was criminally prosecuted by the Circuit Attorney's Office and was acquitted after trial by jury in May of 1998. Thereafter, in June and July of 1998, a St. Louis Police Department Administrative Hearing Officer reviewed charges against Moran. The Hearing Officer recommended to the Board of Police Commissioners that Moran be acquitted on the assault and excessive force charges, but the charges that Moran directed another officer to file a false report on the Bell beating be sustained. The Board accepted all of these recommendations and further concluded that Bell was beaten after he had been subdued by police officers, Moran was on the scene and was in charge at the time and, therefore, Moran was guilty of failing to exercise his authority to prevent the beating of Bell. The Board punished Moran by sustaining his earlier suspension without pay and demoting him to patrolman.

Moran filed suit against eighteen defendants in this court alleging that they conspired to and did violate his constitutional right to substantive due process, and maliciously prosecuted him. Thereafter, Moran took the deposition of Anne-Marie Clarke, President of the Board of Police Commissioners, in which she was asked the following questions:

Q: Do you know Charles Shaw? The judge?
A: Judge Charles Shaw, yes.
Q: Are you social friends with him?
A: Yes.

Q: Has he been to your home?

A: Yes.

Q: How many times?

A: I don't know.

Q: More than ten?

A: No, not more than ten.

Q: Have you been to his home?

A: Yes.

Q: More than ten times?

A: I don't—I have known him twenty-some years. I don't know.

Q: A very long time?

A: Yes, a very long time.

Q: I apologize for asking this question, but have you ever discussed this case with him?

A: Judge Shaw?

Q: Yes.

A: No.

Q: Wayman Smith. Have you ever been together with Wayman Smith and Judge Shaw in a social event of any kind?

A: The three of us?

Q: Yes.

A: I'm sure we have. We are all members of the bar.

Q: Do you know whether Wayman Smith is a close personal friend of Judge Shaw's?

A: I know that we would all, they would be acquainted. I don't believe close personal friends, no.

Q: Were they ever, two of them ever together at your home?

A: I am sure they probably would have been.

MR. GOLDSTEIN: No further questions . . . .

Clarke Dep. at pp. 49-50.

Based on these questions and answers, Moran requested that this court recuse itself from the case. The request was denied.

Following the presentation of Moran's evidence and a motion from defendants to grant judgment as a matter of law, this court dismissed the case. Moran appealed the dismissal and other rulings. The appeal was heard and decided by a three-judge appellate panel, <u>Moran v. Clarke</u>, 247 F.3d 799 (8th Cir.), <u>vacated and reh'g granted</u>, 258 F.3d 904 (8th Cir. 2001), and was reheard by the Eighth Circuit en banc. The full court by a majority of six to four reversed and remanded the case. Among other things, the appellate court directed this court to "revisit and more thoroughly consider and respond to Moran's recusal request." <u>Moran v. Clarke</u>, __ F.3d __, 2002 WL 1446740, at *11 (8th Cir. July 5, 2002) (en banc).

II.

The Recusal Issue

Based upon Moran's request for recusal and the deposition of Clarke, the appellate majority stated the following:

> We are <u>troubled</u> by the record in this case. The district judge's appearance at the same social events as Clarke and Smith brooks little mention. Judges, attorneys and public officials will often share public appearances. This does little to create the appearance of impropriety. The social relationship, however, invites more scrutiny. The image of one sitting in judgment over <u>a friend's affairs</u> would likely cause the average person in the street to pause. That the judge and Clarke enjoyed a <u>friendship of sufficient depth</u> and duration as <u>to warrant several reciprocal visits</u> to one another's homes only <u>exacerbates the problem. We find particularly worrisome the district court's failure to disclose this conflict himself</u>, as permitted by section 455(e). Moreover, the record suggests a fractious relationship between the district

court and Moran's attorneys. We do, however, have
the <u>utmost faith</u> in the district court's ability to rule
impartially, and have imposed on ourselves an obligation
to reverse a district court only where we can say with
certainty that it has abused its discretion. Accordingly,
rather than remand to a different judge, we remand this
question to the district court with the suggestion that
it revisit and more thoroughly consider and respond to
Moran's recusal request.

<u>Moran</u>, 2002 WL 1446740, at *11 (emphasis added).

The majority assumes a conflict exists, but the facts show otherwise.
Neither Clarke nor the undersigned have ever been in each other's homes
on a personal, family or "reciprocal basis." Clarke was last present in
the undersigned's home eight years ago in 1994, when I permitted the
Mound City Bar Association to host a reception for a candidate running
for the Presidency of the National Bar Association. Approximately one
hundred people attended the event in my home, almost all of whom were
members of the bar. Between 1987 and 1993, the undersigned was present
in Clarke's home on three occasions. The first occasion was a Missouri
Bar Association reception in conjunction with the annual Missouri Bar
Conference. The second was a Mound City Bar Association social event.
The third was a birthday party for Clarke's husband, who had been
President of the St. Louis Board of Education. At each of these gatherings,
there were between one to two hundred guests, most of whom were
members of the bar or public officials.

Between 1977 and 1978, Clarke and the undersigned were present
in each other's homes two to three times as part of a group meeting of
approximately half a dozen people attempting to plan and organize an
effort to encourage young African-American professionals in St. Louis
to meet, network and socialize. Subsequently, during this same period
of time, Clarke was present in the undersigned's home for such a social

gathering, attended by more than one hundred people.[1] This court's relationship with Clarke was based on our being members of the bar and of the same small generation of African-American attorneys in St. Louis, rather than on personal matters.

With all due respect, this court's faith in the appellate majority herein has been shaken. While the majority claims to have the "utmost faith" in this court's impartiality, it strongly suggests a lack of faith by stating that it was troubled and worried by "this conflict," which was "exacerbated" by this court's failure to disclose the alleged conflict itself.

Webster's Third New International Dictionary 816 (1965) defines "faith" as a "firm or unquestioning belief in something for which there is no proof" or "confidence: esp: firm or unquestioning trust or confidence in the value, power or efficacy of something." Another authority described it in the following manner:

> [[F]aith is the substance of things hoped for, the evidence of things not seen. For by it the elders obtained a good report.

Hebrews 11:1-2 (King James).

What was <u>seen</u> by the appellate majority was this court's ruling that its relationship with Clarke was insufficient reason for recusal. What was <u>unseen</u> was this court's reasoning for the conclusion. "Faith," and particularly "utmost faith," would seem to require belief or confidence that this court would not reach such a conclusion without a basis. Having such faith, my appellate brethren could have required that I revisit this issue and state my reasoning. Instead, they chose to declare themselves "troubled," and hastily surmised without support in the record that my relationship with Clarke was a friendship of "sufficient depth" that it "warrant[ed] several reciprocal visits to one another's homes." They further found "particularly worrisome" the undersigned

---

[1] The occasions on which Clarke and the undersigned have been present in each other's homes now span some twenty-five years. The occasions referred to herein are all that the undersigned recalls. If there are any other such occasions, they are of the same nature and are not recent.

judge's "failure to disclose this conflict himself." The majority panel's professing to have "the utmost faith in the district court's ability to rule impartially" is wholly inconsistent with its use of such words as "troubled," "worrisome" and "exacerbate." On the contrary, what seems apparent here is an utter absence of faith.[2]

The majority has generated an image of a federal district judge "sitting in judgment over a friend's affairs." This image more than gives one pause. It paints an extremely negative picture of this court's impartiality, and also equates Clarke's service on the St. Louis Board of Police Commissioners with her personal affairs. This picture is all the more distorted when one recognizes that there was no evidence, reference or even a hint in the record that Clarke acted other than as a member of the Police Board in reviewing and acting on the Hearing Officer's administrative recommendation. Full scrutiny of the record would reveal that although Clarke was sued in her individual and official capacities, as were all the Board defendants, she was primarily a nominal defendant in this case, who was not even called as a witness in plaintiff's case. Cf. Gray v. University of Ark. at Fayetteville, 883 F.2d 1394, 1398 (8th Cir. 1989) (district court did not err in refusing to recuse itself from a case in which one defendant, a member of the university board of trustees, had been the judge's law partner five years previously, but was not expected to testify and no judgment would be entered against him personally); see also United States v. Lovaglia, 954 F.2d 811, 816-17 (2d Cir. 1992) (district judge's social relationship with family whose businesses were victims of criminal defendants' violations of RICO did not require recusal where relationship ended seven or eight years prior to sentencing, the judge had no specific knowledge of the contested facts and allegations concerning the social relationship were not "outcome-determinative" in the proceedings). In this case, there is little mention

---

[2]What does it profit, my brethren, though a man say he hath faith, and have not works?

. . . .

[F]aith, if it hath not works, is dead, being alone.

James 11:14 and 17 (King James).

of Clarke in the record other than in reference to her relationship to this judge, with special emphasis on being in each other's homes.

This court recognizes and embraces the established standard for recusal of a judicial officer. Recusal is committed to the sound discretion of the trial judge and a judge "shall disqualify himself in any proceeding in which his impartiality might reasonably be questioned." 28 U.S.C. § 455(a). This issue has been cast as "whether the judge's impartiality might reasonably be questioned by the average person on the street who knows all the relevant facts of a case." In re Kansas Pub. Employees Retirement Sys., 85 F.3d 1353, 1358 (8th Cir. 1996).

It is abundantly clear that the undersigned should have fully addressed his relationship with Clarke on the record in response to Moran's recusal request. The undersigned regrets and apologizes for this oversight. I am mindful, however, that judges, who are "keenly aware of the obligation to decide matters impartially, 'may regard asserted conflicts to be more innocuous than an outsider would.'" Recusal: Analysis of Case Law under 28 U.S.C. §§ 455 and 144 (Federal Judicial Center 2002) (quoting United States v. DeTemple, 162 F.3d 279, 287 (4th Cir. 1998), cert. denied, 526 U.S. 1137 (1999)); see also United States v. Jordan, 49 F.3d 152, 156-57 (5th Cir. 1995) (the average person on the street as "an observer of our judicial system is less likely to credit judges' impartiality than the judiciary"); In re Mason, 916 F.2d 384, 386 (7th Cir. 1990) (lay observer would be less inclined to presume a judge's impartiality than other members of the judiciary).

It is obvious that "all the relevant facts" were not known in this case, yet the appellate majority did not hesitate to decide that there was a conflict. Had the majority acted with restraint and allowed "all the relevant facts" to be set forth before assuming the worst, unnecessary and wrongful damage to the reputation and integrity of a fellow Article III Judge could have been avoided.[3] Was there not leeway for a modicum

---

[3]Good name in man and woman, dear my lord,
Is the immediate jewel of their souls:
Who steals my purse steals trash; 't is something, nothing;
'T was mine, 't is his, and has been slave to thousands;
But he that filches from me my good name

of consideration to be accorded to the district court? Perhaps, on the other hand, allowing this court the opportunity for "more scrutiny" with the suggestion that it "revisit and more thoroughly consider and respond to Moran's recusal request" was intended to be exactly that.

A judge is presumed to be impartial. "Impartiality of course lies at the heart of our system of justice . . . it is what makes the system work . . . ." Denelle J. Waynick, <u>Judicial Disqualification: The Quest for Impartiality and Integrity</u>, 33 How. L.J. 449, 460 (1991) (quoting <u>Judicial Inquiry and Review Bd. of Supreme Court of Pa. v. Fink</u>, 516 Pa. 208, 532 A.2d 358 (1987)). "[T]he law will not suppose a possibility of bias or favour in a judge, who is already sworn to administer impartial justice, and whose authority greatly depends upon that presumption and idea." <u>Aetna Life Ins. Co. v. Lavoie</u>, 475 U.S. 813, 820 (1986) (quoting 3 W. Blackstone, Commentaries *361.) Given this presumption of honesty and integrity, surely there should be room to consider that an error in failing to address a question as to the judge's impartiality is inadvertent. <u>See</u> <u>Liljeberg v. Health Svcs. Acquisition Corp.</u>, 486 U.S. 847, 862 (1988) ("As in other areas of the law, there is surely room for harmless error committed by busy judges who inadvertently overlook a disqualifying circumstance.").

A judge's involvement with other attorneys in bar association activities is not a basis for recusal. Indeed, the commentary to Canon 4 of the Code of Conduct for United States Judges (1999) encourages judges to "contribute to the improvement of the law, the legal system, and the administration of justice . . . . [T]he judge is encouraged to do so, either independently or through a bar association, judicial conference, or other organization dedicated to the improvement of the law." A judge should not be required to withdraw from all social relationships and live in seclusion. <u>See</u> Leslie W. Abramson, <u>Appearance of Impropriety: Deciding When a Judge's Impartiality "Might Reasonably Be Questioned,"</u> 14 Geo. J. Legal Ethics 55, 95 (Fall 2000). Furthermore, it should be common

---

Robs me of that which not enriches him
And makes me poor indeed.

William Shakespeare, <u>Othello</u>, Act 3 Sc. 3.

knowledge, especially among attorneys, that a judge knows many of his or her community's attorneys and public figures. See id. at 95-96. This is even more likely when such individuals are African-American, as there is a much smaller community. This is the reality of public life, which in and of itself should not raise questions about the judge's impartiality. If recusal were required in such situations, a judge might be disqualified from presiding over most cases in which local parties or public figures are involved. Id.

One of the most respected African-American jurists of this nation, former Chief Judge of the Third Circuit, A. Leon Higgenbotham, Jr., when asked to recuse himself stated:

> [A judge] must have neighbors, friends and acquaintances, business and social relations, and be a part of his day and generation. * * * [t]he ordinary results of such associations and the impressions they create in the mind of the judge are not the "personal bias or prejudice" to which the [judicial disqualification] statute refers.

Commonwealth of Pennsylvania v. Local Union 542, Int'l Union of Operating Eng'rs., 388 F. Supp. 155, 159 (E.D. Pa. 1974) (citation omitted). See also, Harry T. Edwards, Race and the Judiciary, 20 Yale Law & Pol'y. Rev. 325, 326 (2002) (quoting Commonwealth of Pennsylvania and commenting that in Judge Edwards' view, to decide cases as well as they are able, judges "should maintain a diverse group of friends, travel widely, give speeches . . . , and seek out opportunities for the exchange of ideas.").

This court finds that as a matter of law, pursuant to 28 U.S.C. § 455(a), its relationship with Clarke is an insufficient basis for recusal from this case. The appearance of the undersigned and Clarke at the same bar association functions or large social events, whether or not hosted in each other's homes, and the several small group meetings of almost twenty five years ago, falls far short of a relationship which would cause a reasonable person knowing all the facts to believe that the undersigned might not be impartial. In sum, the relationship does not require recusal. Accordingly, having reconsidered the issue, this court will deny Moran's request for recusal.

III.

The Racial Issue

This case starts with race, becomes embroiled with race and climaxes with race. The racial context of this case is as follows:

1.   Gregory Bell, a mentally impaired African-American teenager who was mistaken for a burglar in his own home, is seriously injured by the police.

2.   Defendant Chief of Police Henderson, an African-American, publicly apologizes for the mistake and promises to take appropriate action.

3.   During the police department's investigation, a "white sergeant," Thomas Moran, is accused by two police officers (Barry Greene and Terrence DuPree[4]) of striking Bell.

4.   Richard Barry, one of Moran's attorneys, says that during the investigation Chief Henderson stated he wanted "the white sergeant."

5.   After Moran's criminal trial and acquittal and a police board suspension and demotion, Moran files suit in this court, and the case is randomly assigned to the undersigned, an African-American judge.

6.   Moran's attorneys seek to disqualify this judge by inquiring during defendant St. Louis Police Board President Clarke's deposition about her relationship with the judge, as well as fellow board member Wayman Smith, III's relationship with the judge. Both Clarke and Smith are African-American attorneys.

7.   This court denies the request for recusal without explaining its relationship to Clarke or Smith. After the presentation of Moran's evidence, this court dismisses his case.

8.   On rehearing of the appeal en banc, a majority of six white men conclude that Moran established a plausible case of, among other things,

---

[4]Trial tr., Vol. III at 115, 125, 136.

"improper consideration of his race by a police department headed by an African-American." See Moran, 2002 WL 1446740, at *9.

9. The appellate minority of four judges, two white men, one white woman and an African-American man, disagrees with the majority's substantive due process analysis and observes that the majority "introduces possible racial bias . . . into the equation, when Moran neither pleaded an equal protection claim nor alleged in his complaint that any defendant's conduct was racially motivated." Id., at *16. The minority describes the "I want the white sergeant" statement relied on by the majority as "one scrap of testimony that has little or no credibility." Id.

Despite the foregoing, the majority's decision claims ignorance of the racial issue by stating that "[t]he record on appeal does not clearly set forth the race of the various parties and participants . . . ." Moran, id. at *7. It has often been said that justice is blind but the appellate majority appears to embrace willful blindness with respect to issues of race. It is patently obvious which of the primary protagonists in this case are black and which are white. The appellate majority places great weight on evidence that Chief Henderson said he wanted "the white sergeant." Moran, 2002 WL 1446740, at *2. The four dissenting judges recognize that Chief Henderson is African-American. The majority explicitly recognizes that plaintiff Moran is white. Id., at *7. As to Gregory Bell, the majority refers to a May 22, 1998 report of the Police Department's monetary settlement with the Bell family in the St. Louis Post-Dispatch. Id., at *3. This reference, along with the surrounding facts and circumstances of the case, raises an inference that the appellate majority may also have some awareness of Bell's race.

With regard to the race of the judges herein, we all know each other. As to Clarke and Smith, the deposition of Clarke allows for an inference as to their race. Furthermore, Clarke and Smith are prominent, well respected and publicly active attorneys in the St. Louis community.

It appears that the appellate majority may be in denial with its refusal to acknowledge the race of the parties and participants involved, or perhaps wishes to appear color-blind and above issues of race. In any event, the undersigned is at a loss to explain the majority's justification and reasoning for choosing to demean the character of this court with such zeal. The majority goes beyond inference and resorts to rank speculation with regard to this court's relationship with Clarke. The undersigned is left with the deeply troubling impression that had I been white, or had plaintiff Moran been African-American, and all the other facts of this "hard case" remained the same, the majority's opinion on the recusal issue would have been significantly different.

If this court has wrongly inferred that race played a role in the majority's decision, please allow it to apologize. Yet, at present this court remains offended, insulted, troubled and confused[5] not only by the attack on its impartiality, but also by the disparaging tone of the majority opinion, its conflict-supportive word selection,[6] and its

---

[5]The court is confused by the majority's reference to "a fractious relationship between the district court and Moran's attorneys." Moran, 2002 WL 1446740, at *11. The record reflects that throughout the trial, Moran's attorneys persisted in seeking to revisit Moran's acquittal of criminal wrongdoing, despite this court's clear and unequivocal rulings excluding this evidence. Further, although the majority agrees that "[t]his litigation does not revisit [Moran's] acquittal of criminal wrongdoing," id., at *4, it gives probative value to the excluded memorandum of Assistant Circuit Attorney Douglas Pribble, id., at *3, which questioned the merits of the criminal case. Obviously, Pribble's superior, Circuit Attorney Dee Joyce-Hayes, thought differently and decided to seek an indictment and have Moran criminally prosecuted. Id., at *19. In its opinion, the majority cited one of the three newspaper articles this court excluded at trial. See id., at *3. One of the excluded articles the majority neglected to cite was from the March 3, 1998 edition of the St. Louis Post-Dispatch, which reported that Assistant Circuit Attorney Pribble had written the memorandum recommending further investigation. The article states in part, "Joyce-Hayes said Monday that Pribble's memo prompted a thorough re-examination of the case. 'We do not believe the evidence supports (Pribble's) concerns,' Joyce-Hayes said."

[6]For example, the majority disparagingly refers to this court entertaining "only the briefest of oral arguments" on the motion for judgment as a matter of law. Moran, 2002 WL 1446740, at *5 n.4. This court is unaware of any rule or guideline as to the length of time for oral argument, particularly when the court has reviewed a summary judgment motion, conducted a lengthy pretrial conference, and heard all of the plaintiff's evidence over several days. One of the concurring opinions refers to the district court's

"hasty" decision, <u>id.</u> at *13, but four of the ten appellate judges agreed with the decision following careful deliberation.

The majority opinion's discussion of the recusal issue uses words selected to support its conclusion that a conflict exists. The reference to "discoveries" with regard to the court's relationships with Clarke and Smith suggests that these relationships were being concealed. Not all circuit courts of appeal have taken such an approach. <u>See</u>, <u>e.g.</u>, <u>United States v. Lovaglia</u>, 954 F.2d 811, 816 (2d Cir. 1992) (where question of district judge's social relationship with owner of business crime victim arose at hearing and the judge did not specifically mention having socialized with the owner's family, the appellants raised this as an additional appearance of impropriety. The Second Circuit disagreed, noting that the judge discussed his business and legal contacts with the victim's owner, and stated, "[T]he fact that [the judge] did not mention that he had in the past socialized with the [owners] suggests that this relationship did not strike him as important enough to explore and that the social aspect of the relationship was . . . de minimis, or difficult to distinguish from the primary business relationship . . . .").

The majority's use of the term "reciprocal visits" suggests that the nature of the occasions when Clarke and the undersigned were in each other's homes was personal. It is noteworthy that neither Clarke nor the attorney who questioned her used the term "reciprocal" or the term "visit" during Clarke's deposition. This depiction of "reciprocal visits" bolsters the majority's "failure to disclose this conflict" accusation. (It is now apparent from the Clarke deposition that Moran's attorney was seeking to establish the appearance of a conflict, as he did not bother to question her further about the nature of the relationship, once he obtained responses that we had been present in each other's homes. Because the functions at my home and that of Clarke were predominantly attended by attorneys and public officials, it is reasonable to infer that one or more of Moran's four trial attorneys may also have been present or at least were aware of the functions.) It is also noteworthy that the majority failed to mention that Clarke stated in response to a question whether she had ever been at a social event with Smith and the undersigned, "I'm sure we have. We are all <u>members of the bar</u>." Clarke Dep. at 50 (emphasis added). When asked if Smith was a close personal friend of mine, Clarke stated, "I know that we would all, they would be acquainted. I don't believe close personal friends, no." <u>Id</u>. Perhaps the majority felt constrained to be consistent with its commitment to view "the facts in a light most favorable to Moran," <u>Moran</u>, 2002 WL 1446740, at *1, and thereby made inferences that favored Moran. This court was unaware, however, that this standard of review was applicable to requests for recusal.

blatant refusal to acknowledge the race of the participants, much less the underlying racial issues so clearly present in this case.

Over the undersigned's fifteen years as a trial judge, I have strived to be fair and impartial, not allowing race to have an impact on my decisions in this or any other case. Impartiality is the life blood of our judicial system. It is the basis of the respect that our institution enjoys. Clearly "[t]here is no 'race card' to be played in judicial deliberations." Edwards, supra, at 327, 330. The decisions of judges, including the undersigned, should not depend on their race or on the race of parties and participants. We are a nation of laws, not men. Nevertheless, as the dissenting opinion aptly notes, "hard cases make bad law." Moran, 2002 WL 1446740, at *14. The distinguished African-American jurist, Judge Harry T. Edwards of the District of Columbia Circuit Court of Appeals, has observed that "in 'very hard' cases it can be argued that race may at times have a predictable impact on judicial decision making." Edwards, supra, at 327.

IV.

Conclusion

The recusal and racial issues discussed herein weigh heavily on this court's mind. The disrespect that this court feels has been visited upon it by fellow Article III judges makes the orderly administration of justice extremely difficult, if not impossible, in further presiding over this case. This court has struggled with and prayed over its heretofore expressed concerns, and affirms its sincere commitment to its judicial responsibilities, the fundamental requirement of judicial impartiality, and the rule of law. Nevertheless, these concerns have caused this court such extreme discomfort that it is inappropriate for the undersigned to have any further involvement with this case. For this reason, this court hereby recuses itself. Accordingly,

IT IS HEREBY ORDERED that the Clerk of the Court randomly reassign this case to another judge.

/s/Charles A. Shaw
UNITED STATES DISTRICT JUDGE

Dated this 2nd day of August, 2002.